Praise

"This book is a compreher. provides tools and techniques for writers at any stage to develop their craft. Readers of all ages will be inspired, encouraged, and challenged to find their poetic voices."

—**Ian Keteku**, former World Poetry Slam champion

"You Are Poetry is the kind of book that can only be written by a teacher after years of trial and error in the classroom. Mike will show you how to take the ordinary and make it extraordinary by helping students to learn the most important lesson of all, that they matter and that their stories are important."

—**CJ Reynolds**, teacher, author of *Teach Your Class Off*, and creator of the Real Rap with Reynolds YouTube channel

"Poetry has been something I've only recently fallen in love with. I wish I had a book like *You Are Poetry* years ago. Mike not only makes poetry accessible for all, but he gives many incredible activities and resources for you to help others create and understand the beauty in poetry as well. I know I'll be coming back to this book again and again."

—**Todd Nesloney**, coauthor of *When Kids Lead* and director of culture and strategic leadership, TEPSA

"Mike's heart for the poetry in others is clear in every story, tool, strategy, and page of this important resource."

—**Buddy Wakefield**, three-time World Poetry Slam champion and most-toured performance poet in history

"Poetry is one of the ways that we can find our way back to ourselves and our collective humanity, and Mike Johnston's book provides us a way to connect through poetry. Sharing authentically—our pain, our hopes, our failures, our joy, and our love—connects us to others and allows us to see each other and ourselves. This type of connection and the healing that follows from it is needed in every home, classroom, and community. Not only are the resources provided really great for guiding students in connecting with their own poetic voices, but they are an unexpected gift for those educators who may have put their own pens down to paper."

—**Marisol Quevedo Rerucha**, author of *Beyond the Surface of Restorative Practices*

You Are Poetry

YOU ARE
POETRY

HOW TO SEE—AND GROW—THE POET IN YOUR STUDENTS AND YOURSELF

MIKE JOHNSTON

You Are Poetry: How to See—and Grow—the Poet in Your Students and Yourself
© 2021 Mike Johnston

This book is available at special discounts when purchased in quantity for educational purposes or for use as premiums, promotions, or fundraisers. For inquiries and details, contact the publisher at books@daveburgessconsulting.com.

Published by Dave Burgess Consulting, Inc.
San Diego, CA
DaveBurgessConsulting.com

Library of Congress Control Number: 2021931932
Paperback ISBN: 978-1-951600-78-5
Ebook ISBN: 978-1-951600-79-2

Cover design by Goodsoul
Interior design by Liz Schreiter
Editing and book production by Reading List Editorial: readinglisteditorial.com

This book is dedicated to the poet Optimus Prime, who helped me to fall in love with the simple truth that everything and everyone is so much more than meets the eye, that massive stories can be hidden in plain sight in those right in front of us, and that there is infinite capacity in each of us to transform and roll out.

It's the least I can do after my parents threw him away.

CONTENTS

Chapter 4: Pollination
126

Chapter 5: Bearing Fruit and Seeding the Wind
170

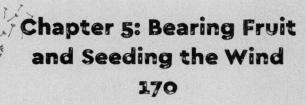

Afterword: Seedlings in the Shade of the Trees
202

INTRODUCTION:

SEE THE FOREST AND THE TREE

"YOU ARE A POET."

It's true. You are, right now, at this moment, a poet who is writing something that only you can ever write by being the only you you'll ever be: something meaningful, authentic, and necessary for people to experience. It is a truth that I hold to be self-evident: all people are created poets.

To best understand my confidence in proclaiming you a poet, it's important to take a minute to understand how I learned I was one. I fell in love with poetry young and built on that relationship as I grew. At the time, I thought I had exclusivity on teenage angst. I, like many brooding teens, would fill notebooks with feelings I felt sounded poetic. These poems were not good by anyone's definition, but putting those feelings down on paper gave meaning and permanence to what I was going through. Something about it felt like proof that I existed.

My words on paper were the bubbles in the water that showed me I was, in a way, choosing to swim over dealing with drowning. It blew my mind years later to find out that other adolescents had been sitting only feet away, spilling out feelings on the edges of notebook pages in the same way. I think back often on those days and wonder what could have been had we all looked up, recognized each other as poets, and shared our stories. It's one of the reasons I believe so fervently in the power of poetry: it is often the voice for those who scribble in silence, when being heard would change everything.

Even as an adult, I wrote. The problem was, when you become an adult, you often feel like the things you spend your time doing have to have some kind of external validation, some kind of value beyond your own experience and enjoyment. People have to buy what we're doing, celebrate it, tell us it was worth that time. Valuable adult time, we're told, has the danger of being wasted. I wish teenage me would have seen the intrinsic value in being able to write with the sole purpose of feeling like I needed to before adult me butted in and questioned if there was a better use for my time. It's like when we become adults and would give anything to have the naps we rejected and didn't appreciate as kids.

Grown up, I sent out poems to be published with great hope. Some were printed, others were rejected politely. I have a drawer full of magazines and books that feature my words and double that amount of rejection letters from projects I wish I could go back and do a little more editing on. One of my favorite ideas about writing is that truly great poems are never really finished, only abandoned. They have to be, because you're always changing, so a piece of writing so personal would invariably want to evolve with you, with how you feel and view things. At one point, the internet was invented, and naturally, I, like most young men unsupervised online for the first time, used this amazing new tool almost exclusively to . . . search out more poetry, especially poems abandoned by incredible writers in every corner of space and time. I unearthed classics and unwrapped modern works. I dove deep into the poetry of hip-hop. And then, there it was, waiting for me: slam poetry.

As much as I had always been in love with poetry, I saw slam as something so much more. It was the story written in constellations I had spent years looking at but was never able to decipher. Now, for those of you who are unanointed in what slam poetry is, let me try to explain it—though I do want to add that I believe it to be the kind of thing you have to experience for yourself to fully imbibe. Nothing I recount will do it justice. It's like having someone describe Matisse's *The Dessert: Harmony in Red* as "a painting with lots of red things and also a lady." Art is always best when you get to interact with it firsthand and allow your neural pathways to solder their own emotional connections.

Slam poetry is all the best parts of poems and performance and competitive figure skating (give or take a harsh Russian judge) made into a gorgeous Frankenstein's monster, sewn together from the best pieces of so many other little things. It is poetry made competitive performance art. All of which celebrates the fact that poetry, like any great art, is about the relationship and connection between those creating and those consuming, artist and audience symbiotically evolving the mood and tone of it all. The judges are always chosen at random, people who happen to be in the venue or walking by on the street. As long as they have no ties to any of the competing poets, they can judge. That, too, is part of the beauty: neither the judge nor the poet needs any kind of training or experience. You score well if you connect well with the audience, regardless of who you are or what you are poeticizing about, which admittedly sounds like some kind of verbal jazz aerobics, which it is, but often involving fewer leg warmers.

The judges give you a score out of ten (with accommodation for decimal points) based on their own personal take on your work. There's also a structure for point deductions if you break the rules of 1) going over your allotted time, 2) using props or musical instruments, 3) using significant amounts of work that is not your own creation, and 4) nudity. Yes, it is a legitimate formal rule that poets are disqualified for nudity, a rule born of an unfortunate incident that nearly lost one poetry slam association the use of their weekly performance venue. You have only your words, your body (provided that it's reasonably covered), and your ability to connect with others as they score you subjectively for that emotional connection. *That* is slam poetry. My own experience in slam poetry is part of how I know you are a poet.

I have seen the power and potential in everyone to be just that, and it all started with me believing I couldn't be. I'd fallen in love with poetry and found the perfect evolution and form of it in slam. I felt like I understood the culture and intention and, as a boy who spent his formative years in drama classes and high school productions, I loved that it was designed to be spoken and presented in my voice. So I wrote, and I practiced, and meticulously chose an outfit I felt made me look the most like I belonged in the slam poetry scene. It had a vest. I went early to the pub where our local monthly Winnipeg Poetry Slam was being held. It was the last regular season event before the playoffs were to begin (yes, slam poetry has playoffs). The sign-up sheet had eight names on it. There were ten available spots. Something inside told me I was a fraud, that even with my poet-looking vest I was absolutely not a poet and would never earn the right to belong to that community. That was until a young man at the sign-up table asked me if I was a poet. Damn. He must have seen the vest, made assumptions, and that's why I was on the spot.

I said, "I guess I am."

Then my inner voice pushed back with, *Really? You are? What makes you say that?* The young man just pushed the sign-up sheet toward me with a smile like an assumption and offered a pen. I took the pen and admitted to him that I was absolutely terrified, felt like I didn't belong there, and that I would likely just be watching the slam from the back of the room, eating nachos and my feelings of regret. It felt safer to identify as a coward than a poet. Another person came in and put her name in the ninth spot with a pen she had in her pocket.

There was my fraud again: real poets must always travel with their own pens. I was clearly out of my league with these writers. The young man tapped his finger on the sheet with raised eyebrows, coaxing me. Still, I resisted. I was standing at the table, talking my way through excuses, when another group ambled in. One of them pulled the sign-up sheet toward himself on the table and, in what seemed like dramatic slow motion, started to pat his pockets for his poet pen. He was going to be putting his name in the tenth and final spot of the night. *There it was*, I thought, *maybe next season.* Maybe by then I could believe I was a poet. But then the young man at the table pulled the sign-up sheet clipboard back and said something that would change the course of my life.

"Sorry," he said, "Mike here is a poet, but we've never heard his story before. We got to hear yours last time, so that last spot is Mike's. I'm just waiting for him to put his name down and give me my pen back."

The man hovering above the tenth spot beamed. He couldn't have been happier for me, despite the fact that I was, in essence, taking the spot he absolutely had every right to sign up for. He was just excited for another member joining and participating in this community, one that made him feel like he was a poet. He turned to me with a meaningful smile and handed me the clipboard.

"Mike. You are a poet. I can't wait to hear your story."

And that was all it took. I was a poet because someone else saw in me that I was a poet. Because this community immediately wrapped itself around that new and untested definition of self and made it feel true. All because someone who knew absolutely nothing about me or my writing knew I was a person with a story, and that was enough. That's how I know you're a poet too. Because someone saw that in me. I see it in you. I see it in my students and colleagues. I see it in your students and colleagues. I honestly see it in everyone. You are a poet. Because a poet is this incredibly simple and simply incredible person that houses a lifetime of stories only they can tell in a voice only they have. Scientifically speaking, there will only ever be one you in the history of this planet, so you have to be a poet. If you weren't, everything your brain and your body and your heart experience would only ever be yours. So, you have to be a poet because your story needs to be shared, and you are the only one who can share it in all of its truth.

Since that night, living the life of a poet has taught me immeasurably about myself. I am a poet. That's part of how I see myself now. But living the life of an educator has shown me that it is so much more than that. As I worked with students, other educators, and all kinds of new poets, I understood that everyone is a poet, but everyone is also a poem. Everyone is poetry. Being both a poet and educator helped me see that we are each an act of poetry. You are a poet because you have influence and choice in how people see you and how you present yourself, while understanding you are so much more than those pieces. You are a poem because you are that condensed form of storytelling. You are so wonderfully complex and so open to interpretation based on the experiences of those interacting with you. You are an act of poetry because you're a process, a balance between what you show the world, what people interpret from the pieces they see, and what they think they see. You are the choices and actions that forge all of that into the shape it will be. You are poetry and poem and poet.

I won that poetry slam on my first night. I won, and I won the next month, and I won until I was the grand slam champion of my province. I won until I went to nationals. I won in Underground Indies. I became a part of an amazing community. In my time, I was the grand slam champion three years in a row. I went almost undefeated during that time. But the real prize was, as a slam poet gaining connections and notoriety and as a provincial and national underground independent champion, I got to tour internationally. Being a slam poet was a huge part of a fellowship I was given through National Geographic that allowed me to run slam poetry workshops in once-in-a-lifetime places with once-in-a-lifetime people, as far away as the Galápagos Islands.

That all allowed me to be in an exceptional position to give back to the community that had given me my identity and so much more. I became the Slam Master of Winnipeg (a bizarrely grandiose title for the person who develops, plans, and runs the events of the local community), I was elected to SpoCan (the governing body of the National Poetry Slam, which is now called speakNORTH), I was cofounder of the Winnipeg Poetry Project, and I was co-chair of the Canadian Festival of Spoken Word. I was the founder of several youth poetry slam festivals and the coach of a few exceptional youth poetry slam teams. I also currently continue to work with National Geographic as a member of their education community, which all came from the seed of slam poetry.

I've had the privilege of working with thousands of students, new poets, and educators over the years. I was asked into schools to work with students from kindergarten to high school to universities and every iteration of education in between. I was a classroom educator by day and a slam poet and poetry educator whenever I wasn't doing that.

I have been from coast to coast eating taters and toast with youth and educators of every conceivable age, race, gender, creed, sexuality, identity, background, ambition, socioeconomic status, country of origin, personality, and style—and the thing they all had in common was this: they were all poets. They were all poetry. Just like you are. Having someone tell me I was a poet and give me the chance not only to agree but to prove the truth of it made two things very clear to me: 1) I was, and 2) it was, is, and forever will be my responsibility to show others that they are too. Which is what I hope to do for you and to empower you to do for your learners. You are a poet. They are poets. You are all poetry. It is already gospel truth; you just have to learn how to preach.

What value do I see in poetry for every student, educator, and person beyond that basic idea of empowerment and seeing themselves as the architect of their own stories? Poetry is the art of valuing and truly seeing people. It is about having both the skill set to communicate the truth of the self and the empathy to understand what others are trying to express. Remember when I said it was easier to identify as a coward than a poet? That was because that was the value I had placed on my story, my voice. Poetry is the acknowledging that everyone has a meaningful and valuable story inside of them as much as it is the medium to give value to that story and voice. It is the synthesis of expression and a means to decode and prioritize emotional information. It's the mathematics of recognizing that everyone has a meaningful, true story inside of them.

So everyone who legitimately sees themselves as a poet gains the skill to decode that emotional information in others. Poetry allows for connection and emotional literacy. It also allows new poets to develop great storytelling techniques. At its core, poetry is a form of storytelling; having the ability to develop and present effective stories covers a staggering amount of the skills we teach in so many curricula. Poetry is a beautiful way to give students (and everyone else, honestly) the means to become language artists and excel in their ability to communicate, both in terms of the emotional information they send out and the interpretation of the emotional information sent out by those around them.

Emotional literacy is an exceedingly important human skill to have. Poetry is a tool in its toolbox.

It is important here, too, to acknowledge and respect that slam poetry is an art form (or the competitive style of an art form) born from Black culture and history. It has roots in roles like that of the griot, traveling poets and storytellers charged with building and transmitting the oral history of West Africa. While today there is an ever-growing number of voices who are empowered by slam poetry, it is important to pay respect to the Black oral traditions that form the roots of it. If you are to take on slam poetry with your community, it is essential that you feature the work of exceptional Black artists like Jillian Christmas and Chimwemwe Undi and Tonya Ingram. It matters to include the work of Black community builders like Dwayne Morgan and Saul Williams and world champion Ian Keteku (whom I'll speak more on later).

Allow yourself and your journey to include this important recognition. There are not only discussions and stories here that are more important than ever, but the more your new slam poets hear, see, and experience, the higher chance they have of seeing and hearing themselves in the poetry—and that is powerful. The more you honor poetry's source, the more you can respect what it has to offer. The same is true for all art forms and the human beings who use them to tell their stories. To speak in poetic metaphor (it's what we do) and keep to our theme in this book, you must feed the roots to grow the rest of the plant. It is important to respect the work of the seed before you let the fruit feed you.

To continue speaking in metaphor, there is a difference between food and a meal (that's not the metaphor yet). Every student is hungry. Heck, every human person is hungry in their own way. Emotional intention, care, and openness all contribute to poetry being the language of feeling, and the fluency of that language changes the things we need as human beings into something so much more. Think for a second about the difference between the last time you ate on the go because you needed to fill a void and the last time you really made the effort to turn food into a special meal, where you dressed up, lovingly prepared family recipes, served it in your best dishes, and talked, laughed, and feasted with people you connect with and care about.

Everyday interactions are fine with passing social skills, but poetry is a tool that can help students and educators alike take the things that feed us socially and turn them from just food into a meal. I will show you how to utilize poetry as a powerful tool for emotional literacy in both yourself and those around you. I will show you how poetry takes the things that connect us and turns them into an absolute feast. There's also a real beauty in finding space to value each and every human story, each and every poem. A great poet named Sarah Kay once said, "Poetry is a house with an open door for you and for everyone around you. It has plenty of rooms; we just need to welcome each other home." I love the idea that each and every story has its own space within a larger community, that each deserves the homage and respect of the experience of a meal rather than simple calories.

So how will this book do that for you? What, pray tell, could possibly present itself as the point and purpose of these printed pages? (We in the poetry business call that a skillful alliteration.) My deepest hope is that you see this book as more than a book. The intention of this book, the very bones of it, were inspired by my eleven-year-old. Really, she inspired this book in more ways than one. She hasn't outgrown me just yet, thankfully. We talk about everything. When she was moving on to middle school and was scared, we talked about that. When I was diagnosed with cancer and was scared, we talked about that. When I told her I always wanted to write a book to explain the power of poetry and storytelling but was scared, we talked about that. She looked me right in the eye and said, "You would tell me to do the things I dream about doing, even if I'm scared, so you should write the book you want to write."

Having an eleven-year-old girl call you out is surprisingly effective motivation. She also inspired the way I wanted this book to feel for you. I want you to scribble in this book. I want you to have it by your bedside. I want it to look dog-eared and awful, full of notes, Post-its, and pieces of you. I want you to put stickers on it and use pictures of loved ones as bookmarks. I want you to want to share it with other educators who care as much as you do, but be reluctant to pass over the copy you've made so obviously your own. I want this book to feel like what writing in journals feels like for my daughter. She puts so much of what she feels, thinks, and dreams into these myriad random writing journals that she leaves scattered everywhere in our house. That's what I want these pages to be for you.

I love that kid, and part of that love is those journals. I love that she values her own feelings and story because she lives in a space where she knows I love and value her feelings and story. I see my students that way more consistently because of her. I see in my students that same innate need to have their story exist somewhere other than inside themselves. As a poet, it has become really clear to me that it's a very human thing to want our stories to exist longer and more meaningfully than the simple cells and scars of our bodies, outside of the gray matter. That's what makes it so important, so essential, that this book allows you to truly identify yourself as a poet and gives you the tools to do the same for others.

You honestly might be the only person who tries to inspire a particular student to put their story someplace outside of themselves. You, alone, could be the one who gives their story the solidity of permanence. Everyone is, either literally or metaphorically, looking for journals to put their story into, whether they are conscious of it or not. Permanency is important. Knowing that other people see, hear, and value the existence of your story is essential. You are a poet. You are because you have to be. You need to care enough about the people around you to tell them the same. You just might be the architect of their shadows, the only source of light that gives them shape and form and shows them they exist.

Not only that, you might be the only person who ever really sees them as their most honest selves, through the poetry they show you they are. As educators, I'm sure we can all think of specific students who we know come to school primarily to be safe, seen, and acknowledged. That's what makes poetry so powerful. It is the opposite idea to computational thinking. It is people-seeing rather than problem-solving.

Poetry has the power to create links between experiences, perceptions, and realities. Where people can feel isolated and marginalized in their stories, feeling like they are alone in what they are experiencing, empowering them to be poets creates connective tissue between them and others, because having a story is what makes us simultaneously unique and similar.

The story itself is unique; the fact that each person is living one is anything but. The very existence of a person's poem, story, and truth is more meaningful for connection than the relatability of the content. Your job is to provide a journal (metaphorically or literally), to give permanence to what students are living, to make them see themselves as poets responsible for and inspired to make themselves a needed and necessary part of a larger collaborative story. Like an eleven-year-old with too many journals around the house, you have to make space for them and help them understand that they are the only poets capable of filling their own journal.

This book and I will support you in doing that in a few ways. Because each poet is unique, I wanted to make sure there was a symbiosis of consistency and flexibility in each chapter. So here is the way the book itself will break down:

First, you'll read this introduction. Look at you; you're doing it right now! You'll also notice that this intro began with the theme of seed and growth. In fact, the entire practical process of this book will follow the natural life cycle of a plant from seed to fully sprouted and all the way back to seed again. It is an apt metaphor for what the book and I will ask you to do. It will be work. It will require growth and adaptation, but it will be worth it, like so much of what we do as educators.

The first chapter and others thereafter will feature (not in a specific order):

- The integration of a classic work of poetry in some way. It will hopefully get you thinking about the theme and activities of the chapter and give you a solid example of something you can reference and work through with new poets to get them thinking in the right direction. It will also help those of you with a more classical poetic bent to see the connection between those poetic masters and the poets sitting in front of you.

- The integration of pieces of slam poetry that do the same thing, only in a more modern and performance-based context.

- An anecdote or two about me and my personal experience with poetry as pedagogy and as a transformative tool that will inject more of my passion into each chapter. This is meant to keep you inspired and help you see the fire in my manifesto, to help you feel connected to my story as a poet so you can add the kindling of my passion to the work and adventures you're taking on.

- You will get practical writing and experiential activities for both you and your new poets. I'm a firm believer in the pedagogy of "I do, we do, you do," so I wanted to make sure you read and hear brilliant poetry in action, try it yourself to develop your identity as a poet and your skills as a storyteller, then extend that to your new poets. It will also help you dive into being a poet and recognize the value of your story. Remember, it's my job to plant that seed for you then help you grow it in yourself, just like it will be your job to do the same for others. Each of these poetry activities will be tiered for grades K–4, 5–8, and anyone else who needs a challenge. That way, no matter who your new poets are, there will be something you can use to help them find their voice and tell their story. I will call these resource sections the "buffet." More on that tasty smorgasbord to come.

- I'll tell you how my story links to yours and to the activities provided.

- We'll spend time in each chapter talking about two terms I have found to be profoundly important in the work I've done and the work I hope we can do together: collaborative storytelling and emotional mindfulness. Each chapter will also challenge you to experience those terms for yourself in a variety of ways.

- Finally, each chapter will interact with the acronym P.O.E.Tree, which stands for pericardial, open, electrifying and . . . Tree (don't worry, I'll explain "Tree" as well as the other less eyebrow-raising pieces soon). It is my hope that this acronym will guide you and help you feel confident that you are using the material as best as you can in the same way PASS (pull, aim, squeeze, and sweep) is a great acronym for making sure you're using a fire extinguisher correctly. I look forward to talking it through with you as a means of quickly checking in with your personal and pedagogical intentions. Both will also help in dealing with the hot fire spit by some of these poets! (That's cool slam poetry lingo, which means the words the poets are speaking; you'll get there.)

Honestly, though, the biggest thing each chapter will feature is you. So much of what we're about to leap into together will be done through the amazing you that you already are. All I can do is write what I've lived and give you opportunities and blueprints. It will be up to you to actually build new poets, stories, and voices. You will have to be brave enough and value yourself enough to make the poem of who you are into the flagship that others will follow into sometimes choppy or uncharted waters. You'll be the exemplar and the guide, the map and the captain, the mouth, the ear, and the heart. You will be the poetry.

I know how much educators love being excited about sharing something meaningful with their learners and new poets on a Monday morning. I can give you the feeling of excitement that comes from seeing another educator online doing something that makes you feel like "Yes! *That's* what my team needs!" but only you can give them you. I will have your back completely as you realize you are a poet, a poem, and poetry. I'll give you everything you need, but you need to plant the seed. Thank you for caring enough to create new poets and see the poetry of yourself. Thank you for being the forest and the tree, the humble imperfect beginning of something and the promise of what it can grow into.

Now, to plant seeds.

CHAPTER 1

SEEDS

"I LOVE MY DOWN SYNDROME."

This is the single most powerful, memorable, yet simple line of poetry I've ever experienced from a student. It was the first line of the first writing share of a festival for high school students I named "Inside Voice / Outside Voice" because half of the conference was about helping new poets find the truth of their inside voice, while the other half was dedicated to turning that into a powerful voice outside of themselves, where they could see the value and need to share that voice. In that moment, I wasn't sure what I had created.

A young man in tenth grade was in attendance among about sixty other new slam poets over the course of the festival, which consisted of several days of writing exercises, sharing, and workshops hosted by Canadian and world champion slam poets. It was intensive, but that was the point: challenging students to become new poets and unearth and share themselves. I didn't know this young man previously. I didn't know any of the student poets. I developed the festival and brought in the experts (those guys I did know, and liked very much), which included teachers and other educators from around the province who had provided me with the students they felt needed or could benefit from the poetry, whatever the reason for that need was.

These students started to write under the expert tutelage of some of the best slam poets on the planet, but this young man wrote very little. He had a full-time educational assistant working with him who took great care to remind each of us that he wasn't going to write much, that he couldn't and that it was beyond him. She reminded me and the team of poets often that he had Down syndrome and wouldn't be capable of much of what we asked of the other new poets, but that he would enjoy the day nonetheless. She told us he just liked getting out of the school for a few days and the bus ride would be the highlight. She told us often how much he liked bus rides. It didn't feel good to me that a grown adult would sip coffee and explain to us over and over the limitations she perceived this young man to have, but this was a time of listening and I didn't want to undermine this professional person who had worked with him daily, so we let him work at his own pace and assisted where we could. Without fail, he kept telling us he was writing a poem and pointing with a knowing smile to the side of his head while she kept telling us he couldn't write much.

She was right. He didn't write much down at all. In fact, he had only written five words. But when writing time was over and we asked for volunteers to share, his hand shot up like a rocket. Like power. Like immediate intention. Like he had something to prove. All eyes and expectations were on him as he delivered the first line of the first writing share, and here was a young man we had been told all morning to not expect much from who was about to sculpt the feeling of the room for the rest of the festival. See, when it comes to workshopping with youth, my experience has taught me that the first share often sets the tone. But this young man stepped up to the microphone and set on fire every-thing I understood about really hearing a young poet. He held the paper in front of himself, breathed in deeply like he was taking every syllable into his lungs, then lowered it slowly, his back powerfully straight, his heart infinitely confident. His stage. His room. His moment. His poem.

"I love my Down syndrome."

Nobody in the room had any idea that was what he had written down. He had kept that to himself. Even though several eyes were already tearing up in the room, he was nowhere near finished. He continued to unfold from heart to mouth this incredible piece of poetry about how he loved his Down syndrome. He loved his Down syndrome because he could always recognize his own face in the mirror when too many other people looked the same. He loved his Down syndrome because everything he did was proof he was more than most people thought he was. He loved his Down syndrome because his mother loved him and saw him as perfect, so how could his Down syndrome be anything but perfect?

There was not a dry eye in the room when he stepped down to total and utter silence after reading the poem he had meticulously written in between and around the five words on the page. Then, the room exploded for him, and I will never forget the powerful feeling of really seeing who someone was to themselves on their own terms and not based on what other people had to say. There is very little more powerful than seeing a person the way they see themselves, even if it's just a glimpse. Because of this boy who loves his Down syndrome, I try to listen with honesty and intention to see who people are through their own retinas and thoughts and tips of their tongues. It is not about how I see them. It is about how well I see how they see themselves. What pieces of yourself do you choose to love enough to speak proudly of? What do you love about yourself as much as this boy loves his Down syndrome?

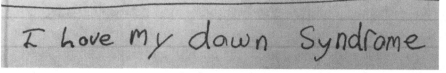

This is the actual handwritten paper that young man created. What do you love so much about who you are that you'd immortalize it on paper?

This chapter is guided by the concept of a seed. Scientifically, a seed is an embryo awaiting conditions of germination. I honestly believe, because I've seen it, that every student, every person, has the embryo of being a poet awaiting germination inside them. I honestly believe that a person's capacity to be a poet is as natural and as much a part of the ebb and flow of living things as actual seeds you can plant in soil and create the right environment for growth around. That's why I am sticking so closely to this metaphorical concept. It goes beyond a way of understanding. Each of us is a seed that has potential beyond what is measurable; we each just need the right conditions to germinate and bloom. Each of us is a poet. We just need the right environment to speak in.

Now, it's your turn to start the journey you'll continue with others. The next pages will include a few handouts so you can print and use them moving forward, but this first venture into writing poetry will be entirely yours. You can choose to print and use the following guides, you can get a journal akin to those of my daughter, you can write on scraps of paper, or you can even write on the inside lips of envelopes like Emily Dickinson. Whatever you do, commit to writing with me. Commit to germinating the seed inside yourself. I often get people who tell me that they don't feel like they're "good at poetry." I see much of this like singing in the car or shower. I do it. You do it. Lots of people do it knowing full well that they're terrible. People don't stop singing because they are aware they'll never sell a single album. In fact, sometimes that lack of pressure makes the singing even more enjoyable. Treat poetry like singing in the car. Or the shower. Wherever. You never need to avoid doing things that you may not be celebrated for. Just sing. Before we move forward together, you will need something to write on and something to write with. I'm serious! Go now before you move on to the next pages. I'll wait!

You can grab a journal or notebook that will be your poetry creation space and a place to put ideas, notes, and feedback, or you can just flip to the back of this book, where I've included some blank pages. Your words, thoughts, and poetry are so important to your evolution and the ways you'll help others on their journey, so when lightning strikes and you need to write things down, flip to the back and make this book as much your poetry journal and inspiration log as it is a how-to manual.

Now that you're ready to put pen to paper, I want to introduce you to an acronym I use with my new slam poets when they write: P.O.E.Tree. Whenever I ask them to write anything, I have them ask themselves this question: Is my writing P.O.E.Tree? P.O.E.Tree stands for pericardial, open, electrifying, tree. I will ask you to check in with this acronym as you go through your writing and poetry education. I want you to challenge your writing and your students' writing to always be P.O.E.Tree.

P—**Pericardial:** I will admit, this one came from the science nerd in me and the work we do learning human anatomy in middle school. I have always believed that science and poetry are synonymous, as they're both ways in which we try to understand ourselves and how we fit into and make sense of the universe at large. The pericardium is the membrane that encloses the heart. It is literally as close to the heart as you can get. I often ask my new poets, "Is this poem as close to your heart as it can be?" Good writing is true and honest, and that requires commitment to being close to the heart of yourself, to your truth. In short, do you honestly connect with what you're doing, how you're doing it, and who you're doing it for?

O—**Open:** Here, we ask ourselves if we're open to sharing those pieces and perspectives of ourselves and seeing other people the way they want to present themselves. If your writing is close to the heart, if you've put that work into your truth, you have to believe that others are speaking their pericardial truth. Poetry is a value system based on emotional literacy and connection. Being open about who you see yourself as not only allows others to hear what you're saying, but it shows them that you're willing to hear them. Remember, this is the antithesis of computational thinking. This isn't problem-solving; this is people-seeing. Are you opening yourself up honestly, and are you open to seeing people based on how they see themselves? Are you the difference between listening and hearing?

E—**Electrifying:** Once we know that our writing is close to our heart and opens us up to connect, we can ask ourselves if the writing we're doing and the way we're presenting it is electrifying. Do you make your process and what comes of it electrifying? Is your poetry electrifying? Really, what we're asking ourselves is whether what we've written and put out there as poets inspires, empowers, and motivates those around us to take up the mantle of poet themselves and, just as important, if it keeps us charged and motivated to build our own poem as well.

T—**Tree:** Does your writing grow, evolve, and get stronger? A tree is a growing thing, putting down roots and stretching to its full potential. It is important to ask yourself if what you're putting out there creates the right conditions for growth in yourself and other poets. It is essential to create poetry that is close to the heart, connects you to others, and empowers and inspires, but all of that is affected by the environment, just like with a tree. Does your truth and poem build an environment where both you and other poets have the nourishment, protection, resources, space, and support that is needed? Imagine everything a seed in nature needs to not only germinate but grow through the seasons, circumstances, and competition for sunlight, space, and nutrients. Ask yourself if what you're building allows for and promotes growth and evolution, for yourself and the poets around you.

Now that you know how to actively reflect on just how much your writing, activities, and interactions with new poets embody P.O.E.Tree, let's get back to the business at hand. You are a poet, after all. It's time to be one. I encourage you to make the following poetry writing activity your own, for yourself as well as your classroom. Write and record however and with whatever medium you like best. Be where you are comfortable. Speak out loud when you need to. Pets make a great audience. Maybe not cats; they're pretty judgmental, but a fish has a three-second memory span, so that's a safe space.

POET ACTIVITY: SEED (HANDOUT)

NAME: _____

WHO ARE YOU?

You are a slam poet!

That's right! You are a poet, and you are already writing a great poem inside you just by experiencing life. Only *you* will ever be able to tell that story. So let's jump in and start finding ways to help you share your poem!

The ways in which you see yourself are lenses that change how you see the world. How you see yourself is important. A doctor, whose job it is to take on the role of helping others, might take on the role of a parent or gardener when at home, and they may feel differently about who they are because of it. Today, you will be challenged to think of all the roles you play and how that affects the way you view and interact with the world around you.

Here's the process:

STEP 1

Please get something to write with and something to write on.

STEP 2

You'll have the option of working solo or with a partner, but groups need to be maxed out at two because this is a timed activity.

STEP 3

There will be a timer, so you'll have to answer quickly! This is the point of the first part of the activity. You'll be asked the same question repeatedly, and it will be up to you to answer it in as many ways as you can, as quickly as you can during the time given.

STEP 4

Once you are finished answering, you will choose a few of your strongest or preferred answers to write with. Here we go!

The question is "Who are you?" In the time given, you will attempt to answer it honestly in as many ways as you can. The more responses you have, the easier the next step will be! If you are working with a partner, you can switch roles at the end of the time. Your partner will ask you the question and will write down your answers as you give them. Remember, it is important to repeat the question and change the answer every time. This challenges your brain to think of a variety of answers. They won't all be amazing, but it's OK; you just need lots of options to choose from.

Some really great answers include "I am a brother," "I am a student," "I am a reader," "I am someone who likes music," "I am a cookie eater," "I am a hater of broccoli," "I am a caregiver to Marvin the goldfish," or "I am a hockey player." Those are just some ideas to get you thinking; your answers should focus on who *you* are!

READY? SET? POEM!

Q: Who are you?
A: I am

_____

_____

_____

Q: Who are you?
A: I am

_____

_____

_____

Q: Who are you?
A: I am

_____

_____

_____

Q: Who are you?
A: I am

_____

_____

_____

Q: Who are you?
A: I am

_____

_____

_____

Q: Who are you?
A: I am

_____

_____

_____

Q: Who are you?
A: I am

_____

_____

_____

Q: Who are you?
A: I am

_____

_____

_____

Q: Who are you?
A: I am

_____

_____

_____

Q: Who are you?
A: I am

_____

_____

_____

Q: Who are you?
A: I am

_____

_____

_____

Q: Who are you?
A: I am

_____

_____

_____

SPLASH ZONE!

If you still have answers coming out, just splash them out anywhere in the space below! Keep at it!

_____

_____

_____

_____

_____

_____

_____

_____

_____

_____

STEP 5

Choose your favorites! As we step into the writing part here, it is important that you pick three of the answers you like the best. Which ones do you feel are the most honest? Which ones would you want people to know about you? How would you want to share your identity as a slam poet with other people? Choose whichever three are jumping off the page.

STEP 6

Remember, this is all about you as a poet! Next, you'll get the chance to write from your amazing and unique perspective, answering the same question based on—you guessed it—the three "I ams" you chose. This portion of the exercise will give you a chance to think about how who you are changes, how you see things, and how only you can ever write your poetry. The world needs it, and it needs you!

STEP 7

You are going to choose a question and answer it three times, focusing as closely as you can on one very specific "I am" perspective. Make sure to begin by using your "I am" answers!

Example (going back to our doctor example from before):

If the question is "What does being in the mall feel like?":

- A1: I am a doctor. To me, being in the mall feels like everyone is sick. I hear all kinds of sniffling and coughing. I see red eyes and skin bumps, and I wonder what I can do to help them. I see little kids, and I hope I never see them in my hospital. I hope they stay safe and happy. I see old people, and I wonder if I could help them if they came in to see me. I see a boy in a cast, and I wonder if it is newly broken or almost done healing. I see people who might need to be fixed.

- A2: I am a parent. To me, being in the mall feels like stress. There are so many people here that I don't know. I care the most about the little one whose hand I am holding. I worry if she will let go of me and disappear into the ocean of people. But I love being here with her. She loves mall food, and I love all the tiny clothing for her. It looks like adult clothing that has been hit with a shrink ray. It's adorable.

- A3: I am a gardener. Man, the mall makes me feel sad. Every single plant here is plastic and fake. I can't water them or grow food from them. I can't care for them. Even the lights are fake. My plants in my garden at home wouldn't like that. They love the warm sun, and so do I. I wonder if they'd let me plant a garden in the main court. There's a skylight there, and the people walking by would love the smell of my flowers.

See? The same person has three very different takes based on the piece of themselves they choose to see the world through! You do the same thing every day, so here is a chance to turn the way you see the world into three unique slam poems about your point of view. In a journal or on lined paper, please take the time to answer *one* of these questions below using your three different "I am" statements.

> **Super Mega Important Note:** Part of being a poet is sharing your words, feelings, and thoughts with people to help them see and feel the way you do, even for a moment. At the end of this activity, there will be a chance for everyone to share a part of their poetry! Be ready to share who you are and listen to and support how other people see themselves. Poetry is a community thing; all pieces and people are needed to make it work!

Here is the list of questions you can choose to answer (remember, you're going to choose one and answer it three times using your three chosen "I am" statements):

- What does the mall feel like?
- What is it like to have a meal with your family?
- What is the most important thing to you?
- What is one thing you absolutely want to do in your life?
- What do you like to do in your spare time?
- What do you think people notice about you?
- What makes you a good friend?
- Do you think you will make a good parent?
- What is the best thing about you and why?
- What animal are you most like and why?

Feel free to suggest additional questions, but please have them approved first!

Modifications: Poet Activity–Seed

I have been a middle school teacher by day and a slam poet by night for over a dozen years now. My personal experience and passion are firmly rooted in middle school pedagogy and the level at which those new poets can interact with this material. I have had the blessing of touring and workshopping with countless students from levels above and below the middle school grouping, and I'm happy to offer how I've modified these same activities for all levels. Believe me, if you're reading this and are unsure if your new poets can handle it, try them. Let them surprise you. Here is how I have modified the "I am" poetry seed activity for grade level and ability.

Primary Challenge:

The K-4 curriculum has a focus on knowing the self, the community, and the connections and roles people have within those spaces. I have found that the most successful way to bring the "I am" activity to younger grades is to collaborate and make the questions more guided.

I put large papers onto the wall that feature traditional jobs of people in the community. For example, I will have a few papers that say "Firefighter," "Police Officer," "Doctor," and "Teacher." It will be up to you to decide what roles resonate the most with your class. I've also had teachers request historical perspective pieces, like "Viking," "Explorer," and even "Dinosaur." Taking the time to consider what is pertinent to your class's study is important when selecting these discussion topics.

Once those posters are up, I ask a few questions that help determine what the new slam poets might know or feel about those particular subjects:

- What do you think they think about?
- What do you think they like to do on the weekend?

- What do you think they like to eat?
- What would you give them as a birthday gift?

I ask them questions until they've filled up the posters with words, ideas, and cues that help them understand the way those people might see the world. Once those posters are filled, I have the new poets tell me, by standing up under the posters one at a time, how they are like or unlike the people on those posters. As they share their thoughts, I jot down what they have to say. Once each student has had a few chances to tell me how they are like or unlike those poster people, I arrange a few of their sentences and read them the poem we've now written together. I have called the poems "Why Our Class Might Be Full of Police Officers," "We Like Roasting Marshmallows, Just Like Firefighters" and "Can You Canoe Like a Voyageur?" The new poets love the feeling of collaborative storytelling. The guided interaction will allow them to dive into the perspectives of themselves and others and allow them to see themselves as poets.

Upping the Poetic Challenge:

When new poets germinate at a higher level, there are ways we can further challenge their thought processes and creativity. For this moment in their process, I use the work of Emily Dickinson. Known for being a poet who found poetry everywhere she could, Dickinson had a book published that only consisted of the poetry she wrote on the inside lips of envelopes she sent to people. Often, these were her "real" poems, the messages secretly intended for the people she was writing to. "On a Columnar Self" speaks to individual strength and is a good chance to have poets ask themselves what makes them strong as they find their voice.

Distribute the poem to them and have them collectively respond to the following questions: What is she trying to say? What does she want you to feel? How do you know this? How does this work apply to the activities you're doing to find yourself as a slam poet? What would you say in response to her? New poets who are able to respond to the work of others while developing their own voice will gain a new perspective as they're working. Studying the work of others while creating for themselves can help build their self-understanding.

"On a Columnar Self" by Emily Dickinson

On a Columnar Self—
How ample to rely
In Tumult—or Extremity—
How good the Certainty
That Lever cannot pry—
And Wedge cannot divide
Conviction—That Granitic Base—
Though None be on our Side—

Suffice Us—for a Crowd—
Ourself—and Rectitude—
And that Assembly—not far off
From furthest Spirit—God—

> Forever -
> is composed
> of Nows.
> —Emily Dickinson

Using inspiration from Emily Dickinson, I always give my higher-level new poets an envelope. As practice and in promotion of the idea that poetry can be theirs, that it exists everywhere, and they are agents of it, I instruct them to write a poem about whatever comes to their hearts. There's no other criteria but that. Then I have them fold the poem, put it into an envelope, and write the "real poem" on the inside lip. That way, they have to make choices about what words, messages, and intentions are most important to send. That's really the essence of poetry: saying the biggest possible things in the smallest available space. It's a fun challenge, and it helps them fall in love with classic poets like Dickinson, as well as the potential and power of the smallest words.

To give you an example of the "real poem" on the inside lip and to further demonstrate the power of a personal poetic truth, I want to tell you about a girl and her love poem. It was a beautiful piece. She wrote about looking at the boy she found attractive and imagining being with him. She used the word "he" over and over. Repetition is a great poetic tool, so nobody thought twice about it. She placed it inside the envelope and wrote the "real poem" on the inside lip. I read the piece, opened the inside lip, and read, "Every *he* is Samantha." It was a simple four-word "real poem" that floored me. Not only had it changed every word of the poem in the envelope entirely, but it sent an immensely powerful message about how this poet felt like the realest parts of her love poems and herself had to be hidden.

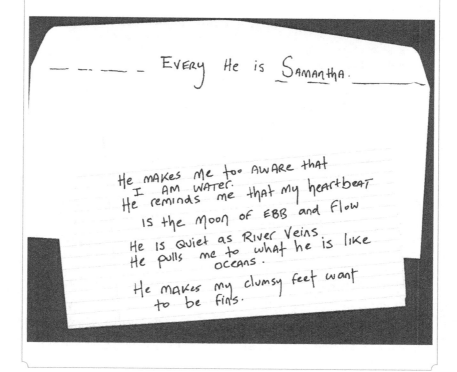

Emily Dickinson used envelopes as a brilliantly romantic way of hiding poetry in seemingly everyday communication. I always ask "advanced" poets, "Where do you keep the secret poetry about yourself, those little pieces of truth within the poem that represent you?" I've had some stunning responses. I have always answered that question with, "In the people around me." What I mean by that is that I try to write little pieces of the poem of who I am on the inside lips of envelopes and in the light in the eyes of the people around me. I try to keep the most honest pieces of my poem and myself in the hearts and hands of the people I interact with. I share it. I use it to help them grow, to build that honesty between us, to write it all together. I believe that the realest parts of my poem as an educator and a father are written in the legacy of the people I interact with, because of who they became around and through me.

Again, I can't stress enough how your open and honest responses in these activities will bring out the most meaningful responses from others. Ask yourself where you write the pieces of your truth. What, to you, represents the inside lips of envelopes? Ask it, answer it, share it, and ask others. Listen. If you listen to where a person keeps those little pieces of themselves, you can start to understand the perspectives they write their poems from.

There it is, the writing activity laid out for your students and new poets. The following activity is for you. This is important for you because I want you to know yourself better and embrace the fact that you are a poet. Your writing will be the example that leads the new poets through their next activity. In the next chapter, we will talk about what that implementation looks like step by step, just like New Kids on the Block taught us, but for right now, this activity is about you. This is your moment of germination.

As promised, every chapter will feature the support you'll need to make these poetry activities authentic to your classroom. If you're an administrator, I want to give you the means to modify these activities in such a way that they can be a part of staff meetings, allowing you to adopt a yearlong challenge to make all of your staff members into both poets and seeds that empower the students' stories and voices. If you're an early-years teacher, I want to give you the tools to help even the littlest and newest poets germinate and create authentically through this activity. I want to empower you to make every educational community one of pedagogical poetry.

I'll offer step-by-step suggestions on how to set up and run these activities from the preteaching stage to a culmination celebration. I'll then follow that up with some grade-level modifications you can make to create opportunities and a space where all of your new poets can express themselves.

POET ACTIVITY: SEED (EDUCATOR SUPPORT)

STEP 1

If the "I Am" handout in this chapter works for your classroom situation, please feel free to make copies for the students / new slam poets.

STEP 2

You can preteach this activity by introducing the idea of what poetry is and why it is meaningful for your students. This will give them a chance to write and present their unique poetry to the classroom and (maybe) beyond! I think it's important to make sure you include slam poetry as a part of your introduction to the poetry you'll be working on, as it is a form of poetry that is really accessible and flexible and will welcome in a whole pocket of potential poets.

Slam poetry is an art form that focuses on presentation and the connection between the poet, the poem, and the audience. Show students really great slam poetry before asking them to create some of their own. Below is a list of what I consider to be incredible slam poetry pieces. You can preview these pieces and make a decision about which one fits your classroom community best as an introduction to slam poetry. I hope you'll be inspired to look through the hundreds of pieces of slam poetry that exist in the word.

- Sarah Kay—"If I Should Have a Daughter"
- Lily Myers—"Shrinking Women"
- Rudy Francisco—"My Honest Poem"
- Andrea Gibson (literally anything they've written)
- Jesse Parent—"To the Boys Who May One Day Date My Daughter"
- Solli Raphael—"Embrace Our Differences" (This is the Australian Youth Champion; it's great for kids to see themselves in action.)

- Los Angeles Team—"Cat Poem" (From Brave New Voices, an amazing youth poetry festival; you'll find all kinds of poems written and performed by some powerful youth to ignite *your* powerful youth.)
- Rhiannon McGavin—"Smile" (another heavy-hitting high school poet)
- Aaron Simm—"Amoeba" (or anything else by this poet; they're my kind of nerdy genius)

I fully advise you to tumble down the rabbit hole here and let yourself find the pieces that make you say, "Yes! This is what my poets need to hear!"

STEP 3

Implement the "I am" activity the way it fits best for your new poets. Make sure to use your own "I am" responses. I can't overstate the value of your new slam poets seeing your unique views and how you see yourself before you ask the same of them. Make it clear before they start the activity that there will be a sharing aspect, and that part of being a slam poet is both offering your voice and supporting the voices of others. Making it a norm early on to share and support is powerful.

STEP 4

The celebration and sharing aspect can take a variety of forms, but it has to be something that is organic to your room. It might look like a morning meeting circle or a stand and speak. For more reluctant new slam poets, I have found success in asking them to share their "five most fantastic words." I do whatever I can to ensure everyone feels like they are a meaningful part of the community, one that would miss their voice if it wasn't heard.

STEP 5 (OPTIONAL)

Depending on how deeply you'd like to make poetry part of your classroom experience, I often celebrate students becoming poets and growing in their ability to share by tokening their accomplishments. On my board, I put up a tree made of crumpled brown paper. It looks legit. Every time we move on to another step of becoming a poet, I give them "badges" in the shape of seeds that they proudly write their names on. They decorate them and put them on the section of the tree they're at. On the following page, I've provided an example of the seed I use and how we place them on the tree. I'll include the others I use as the chapters progress. Each badge will make sense in and around the tree and will allow the students to celebrate their growth as poets.

You should absolutely put yourself up there as well to show them how much you are growing together. You can also have the new poets keep a slam poetry journal in which they can glue these badges as their personal celebrations beside the work they've done. Each time we do a significant activity, I let the new poets decorate their badge, with the instruction: "Make it represent you!" It ends up being a really interesting way to visually track how they see themselves. The final chapter will give you a few suggestions for big community poetry celebrations. These badges could easily be incorporated.

This is the seed I use to celebrate seedling poets! Feel free to copy it, make your own, or get a student to draw one for you. It's a great moment to incorporate science into the lesson!

There is a P.O.E. Tree in my classroom. It is bare at the beginning, but you'll notice there is soil for the seeds (that's where the first badge goes!) then the next badge breaks the surface where the grass is and so on and so on, until you have a really beautiful testament to growing together in poetry. Typically, I have conversations with the students about where they want to place their badges, making sure to ask them not only where they feel they are but *why*. Giving new poets the power to own and justify those choices adds to the strength and validity of their growth.

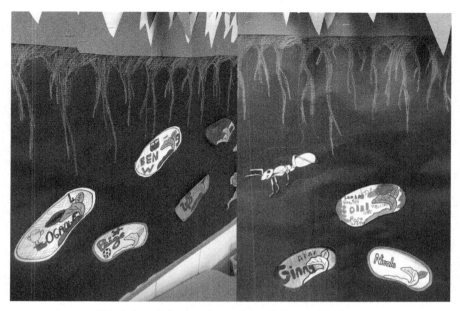

This is how it looks when a few of the seed badges
have been personalized and planted!

Now, put this book down, decide how this "I am" activity works best for you, and write. Be the seed I know you are. Take your time. Keep in mind a young man with Down syndrome who was cocooned in the doubts of those around him, and with so many extra steps to take to make himself heard, still stood up and took the mantle of poet for himself. Imagine what you can do when you've already been told you're a poet, you're now aware that you're poetry, and you've been given the space and support to prove it to yourself and share and celebrate it with others. That is the connection between that story and the activities of this chapter; we as poets need to learn from that young man and dive into our stories and believe they are worth sharing.

Now is your time to start. This piece has to be about you and you alone right now. Make sure your writing is P.O.E.Tree as you go. You got this. And whenever you feel ready to learn how we're going to take this and help your learners see themselves as poets, regardless of their grade level, ability, or situation, you can head to Chapter 2.

Don't forget, you are a poet.

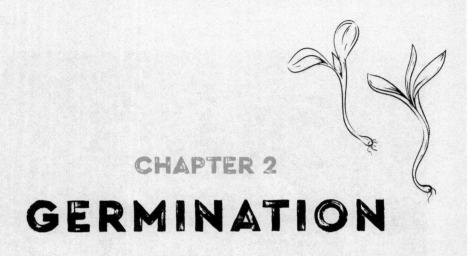

GERMINATION

"YOU'VE GOT A GROWTH THAT IS CONSISTENT WITH A MALIGNANCY."

Not many single sentences have the power to change everything, but that one did it for me. Those words changed the course of what my life looked like and forced me to take a look at who I really had been as a human being. There's something in our life experiences that often makes us feel like nobody could possibly understand what we're going through, that nobody has ever experienced what we are experiencing. Your brain and the systems tied to it will catalog your experiences as completely unique, and it is incredibly important to remember that when you're interacting with someone else, their life experience is also unique. Everyone's experiences are impossibly important and meaningful. You are the only you, the only poem that will ever be written by your moments and emotions.

I know, it sounds very Mister Rogers, but the science is solid. A life's experiences cannot be duplicated. That can make any person feel justifiably isolated when the biggest things happen. We can work to avoid this by acknowledging it and seeing human connection less as putting yourself in someone's shoes and more like connecting their dots to your dots until a picture starts to form. Stay in your shoes. Nobody wants to wear them. They won't fit right. Instead, ask people what it feels like to wear their shoes and walk their path, then listen and connect. This is all about seeing and celebrating people walking miles in their shoes and finding ways to walk beside them in yours.

Hearing how they perceive their walk is so much more important than trying to interpret it. This, unfortunately, always makes me think of a terrible Nicolas Cage film called *City of Angels,* in which he plays an angel who gives up his immortality to stalk Meg Ryan after becoming infatuated with her while he was invisible. There is a scene where she is eating a pear, and he asks, "What's that like? What's it taste like? Describe it like Hemingway." Meg Ryan responds, "It tastes like . . . a pear. You don't know what a pear tastes like?" and he answers, as his hairline recedes even further, "I don't know what a pear tastes like . . . *to you.*" Don't watch this movie; it is not good. Instead, think about the importance of that idea. There is so much power on both sides of a relationship when you understand that it isn't your job to interpret and understand another person on your terms; it is your responsibility to empower and inspire them to share their experiences as their own, because only they (sigh) can tell you what a pear tastes like to them. Imagine how much of Meg Ryan's moment would have been lost if he had just said, "I, too, have eaten a pear, so I know exactly the feeling of your experience. Let me tell you how I think you feel about pears." That sends the message that validating your own empathy and understanding is more important than creating space for the other person to share their perspective in their own voice.

"You've got a growth consistent with a malignancy" was the pear I felt only I had ever tasted. To clarify, my doctor had just told me I had cancer. He said it was aggressive and that I'd have to immediately have surgery to remove the parts of it that could be removed. He said once I recovered, I would almost immediately have to have chemotherapy to kill off any remaining cells. That's when I felt the tremendous gut punch of solitude. I honestly believed, in those moments, nobody could possibly understand how I felt. To be clear, I had been, and continue to be, supported in absolutely every second of my cancer journey by the people who love me, but it still felt so lonely. Life had never felt more quiet. I had never had more walls up around me to protect the people I love from having to go through it with me. Even with all the love and connection my family gave me, it felt like I was alone in the experience of having cancer. I couldn't put it into words because I felt like words had never previously existed for it. Then, I started to write. I wrote about how cancer and losing pieces of myself felt. I wrote about how fear felt and how my new relationship with mortality felt. It felt powerful to personify my cancer as hungry and evil in writing. It felt meaningful to be able to describe how my entire body felt like a stranger.

Losing my beard was surprisingly big for me. I felt so ashamed to face my son without it, knowing I would look like a stranger to him for the first time. But the day it fell off my face, I picked him up from school. I got to my knees, and he looked at me with confusion for only a minute. Then, he looked me in the eyes, smiled, touched my new smooth face, and said, "Hi, Daddy. It's OK your beard fell off; you're still handsome." Of course, I lost it after that, bawling in public and bear-hugging him like I didn't have several hundred pounds on him. He reminded me that I was still me, still the author of my poem. Writing down those feelings and moments turned cancer into a series of stanzas. Cancer became a poem I was writing. There was power in telling people how the pear of cancer tasted to me.

Only later did I feel the need to develop my feelings into real slam poetry. Eventually, I went out to slams and open mics and started to share my story. It was selfish. I needed to share it. I usually do slam poetry with the intention of connecting to as many people as I can in the room, to wrap us together in experience and make us feel less alone. But that time, I shared without any expectation of connection, only with the hope of being heard and understood. That was, until they started to come out of the woodwork. Every time I shared poetry about my cancer, people came up to me afterward to share their own cancer stories with me. It was impossible for them not to tell me about their cancer, their loved ones, people they lived and fought with, people they lost, people they didn't.

It was then that I understood the pear. We are not responsible for imagining ourselves feeling what others feel. We are responsible for being an honest seed, sharing our truth, and letting that be the thing that convinces the seeds around us to do the same. It's not about common experience; it's about caring enough about the human beings around you to share your immeasurably unique self, then giving them space to do the same. Cancer never made me alone, but it also never made me connect. Each story, while it included cancer, was so beautifully unique and wonderful. Knowing that I had my own story in a sea of equally individual and important stories was the connective tissue. We are all the same in that we are all unique. All it took was a seed, and being open in both directions was what made it germinate.

This chapter is inspired by the concept of germination. Scientifically, germination is the idea of something coming into existence and developing, a seed or spore that, given the right conditions, can become the first inches of something more. In Chapter 1, I talked about my deeply held belief that there is a poet inside everyone, dormant, awaiting the right conditions to break seed and grow. I challenged you to break your own seed and give your new poets the inspiration and opportunity to do the same. I honestly believe the path of a poet follows the same path as a plant. Here, in germination, I want to offer you the stories and activities that will allow you to help your little seeded poets grow and evolve. That is how my story will inspire the following activities and intentions.

But wait! This chapter features an exciting two-for-one charming anecdote! I have long considered myself an ally for the incredible LGBTQ+ community. Allyship is something that changes and requires meaningful work. It isn't just about attending parades and rallies, as important and fun as those big moments are. I read, listen, talk, learn, and make space as much as I can to constantly evolve as an ally. My LGBTQ+ students, friends, and family deserve that from me, and so do yours. Poetry is a brilliant forum to give space, listen, and learn. I've always been inspired by just how much passion and fight there is within this brilliant group of human beings to have their stories heard and be willing to take on so much for the right to be seen as they truly see themselves, to exist unabashedly as who they know they are. It is stunning, and I have used my podium within the poetry realm to speak as often and as loudly as I can about these voices, the human rights of dignity and family, of being able to safely be who you really are, and loving by your own definition and lens. It is important to recognize the privilege that exists in being a person like me who has never had to fight to simply exist on their own terms.

Once, in a national slam competition, I performed a poem called "Straight. White. Male.," in which I called out my privilege and spoke passionately about the human rights issues woven into the LGBTQ+ movement. It scored very well, and I ended up winning that section of the competition. Another incredible poet had spoken her piece about having to be too quiet about the love she felt for another woman because, as she put it, "there's too few comfortable ways to start a great love story by double-checking to see if someone is gay when you run into them at the grocery store." I had never really thought about the assumptions I had made in my own awkward flirtations. It was a powerful and beautiful piece. She didn't score as well as I did, she didn't win, and she wasn't celebrated that night in the same way I was. Now, I love this person. She is a dear friend, and I was baffled why later in the evening she wasn't really happy with me. I am eternally grateful that she had the heart and cared about me enough to explain why.

"People heard you more as a straight ally than they did me as an actual gay kid. For all the things I'm fighting for, I shouldn't have to fight for more space in a room full of people who actually came here to listen to people tell their stories. Being a vocal straight ally to a gay kid shouldn't ever have a higher social impact than being an actual 'fight every day for who I am' gay kid."

She was absolutely right, and it changed the way I approached working with students and educators as a slam poet. It changed how I viewed this germination piece. Yes, your story has to be the seed and that has to awaken the seeds of others, but germination is about growing the things that break seed on their own conditions and terms. A seed doesn't germinate and grow because you tell it you understand what environment it needs; you have to see its needs and build around them. This is the important difference between creating equity and seeking equality. If you ever find yourself giving your take on an experience that isn't yours like I did, or if you ever find yourself trying to speak about how passionate you are about supporting a story you haven't lived, just breathe for a minute and ask yourself, "Is this my poem? Or is this a chance for me to advocate by clearing space for the voice of that lived experience's truth?"

Equality isn't the goal in terms of space. Equity is. Certainly, every voice is important, but each will have different needs in different moments. As a straight, cis-gendered man, stories of people like me make up too much of history. People need to see themselves represented in the world around them to imagine what they can become. When choosing poets to showcase and poetic resources to use, remind yourself that your poem is important, but there are poets around you who will only break seed and germinate if they feel there is space and sunlight for voices like theirs. Seeking that balance is what really brought to light two massive terms for me that have guided my practice as a poetry educator: *collaborative storytelling* and *emotional mindfulness*.

COLLABORATIVE STORYTELLING

Collaborative storytelling is a term that has really guided my practice and allowed me to achieve some level of balance between my poem and the poem I am asking others to write. We as human beings approach things with our own lenses; it's only natural. When it comes to collaborative storytelling, I try to be aware of my lens and take further steps. What I mean by that is, if we put effort into acknowledging our unique perspective and its inherent bias, we can do a better job of managing how that lens influences our participation in the world around us.

Dr. James Comer wrote, "No significant learning can occur without a significant relationship." Being a slam poet in a room full of other slam poets, each vying to write their own poem, requires an appreciation that this is the case. But George Washington Carver, the maestro of all things peanut-related (did you know he dreamed up over 105 uses for the peanut?) really clarified the bedrock of collaborative storytelling when he said, "All learning is *understanding* relationships." Collaborative storytelling is a beautiful Frankenstein's monster of these ideas. There need to be significant and meaningful relationships, you have to understand those relationships, and you need to know yourself and be open to real and authentic understandings.

In essence, who you are influences who the people around you feel they are and who they believe they can become in your presence. You need to understand that you influence their story, and they influence yours. You are a lens through which they can see themselves. Each of your relationships and their impacts will look unique. Embrace the idea that every line of the poem will be an exercise in the give and take of understanding. Some new poets will need a ton of coaxing and support; they will need you to make them feel absolutely safe and secure before they share pieces of themselves. Then, once they give you a little crumb, you'll have to work hard to celebrate and grow that piece with them to create space for more.

Your relationship with them will allow you to create the environment that is right for their germinating poet self to grow. While it should always be their voice and their poem, it is essential that you embrace the collaboration they'll need to feel effective in telling it. Sometimes they'll flourish and bloom with nothing more than your listening ears. Others will need you to help them find the confidence to grow their voice word for word. Care about them enough to take the time. Be intentional with every line and every inch of every relationship in your collaborative storytelling. Know that they need you to help them feel capable and valued as they write. I promise you it will be worth it. To be clear, my take on collaborative storytelling is that it is a supportive/receptive philosophy, a mindful understanding that everyone impacts the stories and the telling of those stories within one another. It is so much about symbiosis for me; all of our stories and poems naturally give and take from those who are actively engaging in one another's lives. To slightly modify a famous Spider-Man quote, it is both a great power and a great responsibility.

EMOTIONAL MINDFULNESS

The essential sidekick to collaborative storytelling is what I like to call *emotional mindfulness.* When we're asking our students to be poets, to be honest with themselves and with us, we have a responsibility to be exceptionally mindful of the emotional content flying around the room. What we're trying to create here, in essence, is a murmuration of slam poets. If you're unfamiliar with the scientific concept of a murmuration, please stop reading right now and google it. I'm serious; put the book down and seek it out. I'll still be here. Take your time.

Beautiful, right? A murmuration is hands down one of my top five favorite scientific happenings. A murmuration is when a group of hundreds, sometimes thousands, of small birds fly in a massive cloud that ebbs, flows, and changes, with the movements of each bird connected to the movements of the birds around it. It is a living cloud made of birds, the perfect marriage of chaos and control, of physics, intention, and reaction. It is considering the existence of those flying beside you while still making the movements instinct tells you to make. This whole exercise is about giving new poets the means to find their authentic voice and write their stories in the safety of a community. I can think of no better metaphor for that than a murmuration, where so many little birds are moving in their own directions while being mindful of the movements of the others around them. It is the perfect physics of the individual moving in harmony with the collective for both individual and collective intentions.

What that means for you as an educator and a member of the larger murmuration is that you have to lead the charge of emotional mindfulness. You need to show your authentic self, as well as promote, see, and value the authenticity of the poets around you. This is not always going to look positive. Some stories are harder to tell than others. But you possess an opportunity here; you have a group of new poets who are looking to you, looking to your heart to lead theirs. Feelings can be fallible and dangerous. New poets might bring things up that are hard for others to hear; they might surprise you and each other. You need to honestly look and listen to each and every poet and help them create that sense of safety within and around themselves. Take the time to ask if your germinating new poets are getting what they need to move to the next stage of growth. Sometimes, that looks like laughing with them; other times, that makes you the shoulder to cry on, but all the time, that makes you the one who is the most emotionally mindful in the room. You're the reason a murmuration will be a beautiful tapestry of individual movements rather than hundreds of starlings colliding midair.

"Mike! I'm only one person, and my learners are too diverse in their needs and abilities to be collaborative storytellers!" That's a fair point, but there are a few very important things you need to remember:

1. All you need to do to be an emotionally mindful collaborative storyteller with your new poets is care about them enough to really listen to and consider them. You're more capable of that than you know. You're an educator.

2. I promised I would provide you with step-by-step assistance and resources to help transform your classroom or school into a poetry community full of self-identified poets. That's how I believe we can create a beautiful murmuration. You've got them, and I've got you.

3. Don't put pressure on yourself to be all things to all new poets. You are you, and that is something huge already. Do what you can. Remember, this is a partnership with your new poets. We manage best when we manage small. (Or, as the title of Linda Gregg's 1942 poem says, "We Manage Most When We Manage Small.")

POET ACTIVITY: GERMINATION (EDUCATOR SUPPORT)

STEP 1

Make sure you have completed the "Who are you?" activity from the last chapter before getting started. Sharing your own story will open you up to your students and give them a great example.

STEP 2

Make a plan that fits who you and your soon-to-be poets are. Making all of this authentic to your classroom is paramount. After you've done your own "Who are you?" piece, take a minute to think about the new poets you'll be working with. What do you think they'll need? What do you think will motivate them most effectively to break seed and bloom? How do you make this experience P.O.E.Tree for those you're asking to become poets with you? This is the step where you build a poetic plan of attack that fits your classroom best.

To grow at the pace and in the vibe you feel is right for you and your new poets, you have to make decisions about what this will all look like for you. For some of you, this might look like having a P.O.E.Tree on a board in your classroom to plant student seed badges. For others, it might look like getting together in a circle and asking your poets what they want this experience to entail. Make sure it is P.O.E.Tree.

P —PERICARDIAL

If it's done right, this will create a murmuration, a beautiful movement of individuals and the group at the same time. Ask yourself how you are making sure every new poet has an opportunity to be as close to their heart as possible. How are you making sure they feel safe exposing the layers closest to their hearts in the space you are building? How are you showing them you really care about their voice?

How will you make your space and experience pericardial?

I will. . .

_____

_____

O —OPEN

This will be about seeing new poets in the ways they are asking to be seen. As you're setting up this plan, it is essential that you ask yourself how you are personally going to make sure you hear their truth and allow yourself to see them as they want to be seen, not as how you've learned to see them. How will you promote the idea that every poet deserves to have an audience that will hear what they say with true openness? Listen, don't just hear. Validate and value their truth. I have seen students change how others saw them completely because of the community's openness to listen. Remember, you set the emotional tone here.

How will you make your space and experience open for everyone's individual truth?

I will. . .

_____

_____

_____

E —ELECTRIFYING

Part of being a great educator is asking yourself every day how to inspire, empower, and motivate learners to interact with the material in authentic and meaningful ways. How do you plan to keep their batteries charged about the poetic work of evolving self-perception? There are few things more electrifying than being given the power to self-discover, knowing someone is waiting to listen honestly and openly.

How will you make sure lightning keeps striking where it needs to? How will you set up your lesson plan to make sure your new poets' hearts are charged enough for whatever length of time you've decided on?

I will. . .

_____

_____

_____

T —TREE

These are really the questions this section boils down to: What is your plan to ensure this isn't just a one-off lesson? How do you want to structure this and present it as a living, breathing moment where learners will see themselves as poets and grow and evolve through that? How are you going to make your environment one that promotes growth and strength and nourishes your seedlings?

How will you make sure the poems and the people writing them have all the motivation, validation, and inspiration they'll need to grow and make this bigger than themselves?

I will. . .

_____

_____

_____

Things I want to remember when mapping this out (Notes to Self):

_____

_____

_____

STEP 3

Buffet time!

You've put in the work to make yourself the flagship poet of this experience, and you're ready to put yourself out there. You've been emotionally mindful and made a meaningful plan to invite your learners to be new poets with you and participate in some collaborative storytelling. You are the best set of eyes and ears, the best heart and mind, to understand and develop the most meaningful plan for your slam poets. I want to make the next step fun and give you a wonderful tickle trunk full of resources you can choose, use, modify, fortify, or adapt. I want this to be practical and accessible for you.

Making a plan through the buffet is your doorway to be both brick and builder in all of this. Buffets are the only places where it is socially acceptable to try little bites of everything or pile your plate high with the things you know you love. This book will lay out the pieces to plan single activities, entire units, and yearlong community poetry projects. It'll be up to you to "Frankenstein" this smorgasbord into something that looks and feels like the right kind of monster for you. How much time do you plan to spend on the lesson? What is your end goal? What are you trying to get students to create for themselves?

Next, germinate the new poets. Show them the power of their voice when it is legitimately heard. Scientifically, nothing in nature exists alone. Nothing. Use the fact that you are connected to the new poets around you to activate the poetry that is already seeded inside each of us. Finally, share, celebrate, and help them become agents of germination themselves.

Welcome to the buffet! This section is full of resources that are appropriate for wherever you and your new poets find yourselves. For example, with this being the germination chapter, the following activities are designed to spark brand new poets and get them trying new things, building perspective and confidence.

I wanted to make an important note here in the first of several buffet sections. These are built for you to be able to pick and choose certain resources to develop your perfectly organic experience from start to finish. For some of you, this might look like a poetry week of unit learning. That's fine; there's plenty in here for that. Others might choose to make this a yearlong endeavor where you plan for an amazing culminating event. That's why I've made sure to include some amazing larger-scale culminating events and activities in the final chapter's buffet. I mention this now because you might be, as I am, someone who likes to plan with the end in mind. Please feel free to skip all over this book, going to the final buffet, getting excited about a culminating event, then coming back here to fill the space with all of your favorite tasty poetry treats!

BUFFET BREAKDOWN
(ANOTHER OFFERING OF DELICIOUS ACTIVITIES)

1. **Who Are You?**—You already have access to this activity in a previous chapter, but I wanted to mention it anyway as a great potential starting point for all of your poets.

2. **Poetic Specs**—This writing activity will challenge your new poets to look at the world around them more poetically and share those perspectives.

3. **Poetic Snapshot**—This activity allows new poets to start rounding out and solidifying how they see themselves and offer this perspective to others poetically.

4. **Fill in the Poem**—This activity is a way for new poets to create and have fun with poetry that is both deeply personal and has the safety and structure of a fill-in-the-blank writing style.

5. **Dream Like Langston Hughes**—This analysis and writing-based activity will allow new poets to learn how to use their five senses to make unique individual experiences relatable through shared sensations.

6. **Photobomb Slam Poem**—This activity helps new poets practice the art of creating poetry through their experiences and specific emotional perspectives. Using photos they've taken as a basis, it is a way to both share and seek stories.

7. **Paint Swatch Poetry**—This activity teaches new poets about emotional intention and responses from the perspective of colors, something that can be both universal and unique.

POETIC SPECS—GERMINATION

You are a poet! But how do you even *be* a poet? Poetry is a compressed form of literature. That means it might be small, but it has a lot to say and express (just like you). It is a carefully chosen set of words that express a great depth of meaning. In other words, poetry is about trying to get big feels and understandings across in a small package! One of the best ways to do that is to use the power of simile and metaphor. This helps people understand what something looks and feels like to you.

Simile	Metaphor
A simile uses the words "like" or "as" to compare two things. Ex: Sadie swims like a fish.	A metaphor is a comparison that does not use the words "like" or "as." Ex: Meg's mind is a computer.

In the sentences below, what is the writer *really* looking at? What are they comparing the object to? Let's see if we can figure it out! Write what you think and do your poetic best!

Main Object		Comparison
	Her feet peeked out from underneath her long jacket like little mice.	
	The trees lunge and plunge in the breeze like an elephant's trunk.	
	Little black birds glided in loops and swirls like skaters that skate over the frozen river.	
	A man at the mall, his hands full of shopping bags, pushed through the crowd like a boat moving through waves.	

How did you do? Let's compare and chat. How did these make you feel? What images did you see in your mind when you were reading them?

Now, it's your turn. It's time to put on your poetic specs and get writing! On the following page, there will be images and ideas to the left and space on the right to be as poetic as possible in comparing those things to something else. This will help other people understand what you're experiencing and feeling. That's what great poets do!

All right, poet, time to get to it! If there isn't enough space for your creative genius, use a sheet of loose-leaf paper.

What You Are Really Looking At	What It Looks and Feels Like Through Your Poetic Specs
The moon peeked behind the branches of the trees . . .	*I'll give you an example for the first one, then it will be your turn, poet!* . . . like a prisoner behind cell bars. *Now, you try!*
Smoke rose from the bonfire . . .	
Kids lined up at the bake sale . . .	
Fans raved at the basketball, football, or hockey game . . .	
People suntanned on the beach . . .	
High school kids partied at a school dance . . .	
The garage sale became busy . . .	
The mall filled with shoppers during holiday shopping . . .	

The zoo animals arrived for feeding time . . .	
The movie theatre emptied right when a movie ended . . .	
You opened the window where you live . . .	
The people at the water park or swimming pool moved around . . .	
The feeling of being on a road trip was . . .	
[Doing your favorite activity] was . . .	
Plants grew in a garden . . .	
The feeling of the museum after closing time was . . .	
Your teacher's desk looks . . .	

Now choose your absolute favorites. Which ones made you laugh? Which ones did you feel like you did a great job on? Which ones made you feel like a real poet? Be ready to share like the poet you are. People need to hear your genius!

Modifications: Poetic Specs
Poetry Activity–Germination

Primary Challenge:

The K–4 modifications for this activity work for older new poets as well, as they are movement based and you never outgrow the need to move, shake, and have a little fun. For this activity, I choose a series of simple images (animals, foods, items of clothing, vehicles, etc.) and either project them or put them up on chart paper. I ask the new poets to get up and move around the room like each of the images. Asking them to move like a mouse, for example, results in them skittering around the room. This integrates dance and the dramatic arts into the lesson. Then, they sit and I ask them to describe how they moved. I ask things like "How did it feel when you were moving like a mouse?" "How does a mouse move?" and "What do you feel when you see a mouse?" Once I've documented all their words, thoughts, and ideas that will help guide them, I ask, "What else is like a mouse, and why?" Because kids are amazing, I've gotten answers like "A mouse is just like a quick little remote-controlled car because it makes you jump and lift your feet fast" and "A mouse is like my little brother because he zips around the house and loves cheesy cheese."

Upping the Poetic Challenge:

This activity modification is great for new poets who need a more substantial opportunity to ask important questions about the human perspective. Together, we ask how each person's unique lens on the world not only gives them a set of built-in tools to write with but has already helped them start writing it.

I offer a phenomenal piece called "Geraldine Moore: The Poet," which is a short story written by Toni Cade Bambara that provides a great starting point for new poets who need more of a challenge in perspective. The story is about a young Black girl who is living an exceptionally difficult series of life events and can't find the space in her life to complete her school assignment of writing a poem. In the end, writing about her life makes her teacher feel like she's heard the most honest and beautiful poem. This is also a great place for discussions on race and the education system.

We read this piece together, and I have the students really push their poetic specs. We break down the short story and talk about it thematically and in terms of the writing tools being used, then I challenge them to *be* Geraldine Moore. I challenge them to take their audience through a day in their lives in poem form, with respect to the tone and mood their piece will bring. Another activity I offer you later in the chapter (Poetic Snapshot) will offer something similar but more structured if you like this idea but feel it is too heavy in expectation.

Mega Meaningful Additional Addition:

I see this chapter as a way to help new poets discover their voices and learn that there is value and importance in their story and perspective. At some point in our intro activities, I ask them, "Why are you the only person that could ever tell your story?" Often, I have them write that question at the top of the page then write as honestly as they can, answering the following questions:

- Why are you the only person who could ever tell your story?
- Why does it matter?
- Why do people need to hear it?

This is where we uncover how meaningful slam poetry is as a presentation style, especially if it means finding something authentic for your new poets and community. Here are a few solid examples of slam poets who speak their truth in their work:

"To This Day Project" by Shane Koyczan: This is not only a great piece but an example of some of the more visual poetic aspects your slam poets can choose to undertake, perhaps as a culminating activity.

"What Kind of Asian Are You?" by Alex Dang: This is a piece that speaks to the importance of individual experiences. It is essential that you choose pieces that will allow new poets to see and hear themselves reflected in the work.

Sonya Renee Taylor, Megan Falley, Denice Frohman, Gayle Danley, Sage Francis, Hanif Abdurraqib, and Carlos Andrés Gómez are a few more incredible poets. There are so many beautiful truths out there. Embrace the discovery of them!

This next activity, paired with the "Who Are You?" prompt, is a solid basis for germinating new poets and giving them the tools to start speaking their truth. Below, I'll walk you through how I have modified these activities for younger or higher-level learners.

POETIC SNAPSHOT

Poetry is all about bringing someone an experience, a feeling, or an idea with a concise and specific set of words. To start exploring the idea of taking something huge and meaningful and condensing it into a single moment, take the thing you know best (yourself) and transform it into a one-shot, twenty-five-words-or-fewer experience. The idea is that a complete stranger could walk by the snapshot and understand who you are and what it would feel like to be you! Be sure to consider as many aspects of yourself as you can. What do you love? What is important to you? How would you describe yourself physically? Emotionally? As a person? What do you believe in? What do you like to eat and do in your free time? What does your family look like? What do you care about? What do you fear? What do you want to be when you grow up? (Feel free not to.) Try to encompass everything people would need to know to understand what it's like to be you. Give them all they would need to step into your shoes and skin for even a second.

You will be expected to include at least one visual of yourself and another visual that means something to you. You will be expected to write phrases that are exactly twenty-five words or fewer. You will cut them out and paste them around the picture of you, creating a snapshot of yourself. Within those twenty-five words, you will be expected to include at least five verbs, five nouns, and five adjectives. The final ten words will be up to you.

Feel free to choose nouns, verbs, adjectives, adverbs, other languages—whatever is most authentic to you! Points will be awarded for the visual elements, organization, and overall appeal of the piece you put forward. Feel free to include any other visuals, drawings, or collage aspects that build the experience of you. Remember, the biggest goal is to have a single page that takes someone into the experience of what it feels like to be you.

RUBRIC

This rubric can be used by either an educator or a new poet because each piece is a solid opportunity to review and reflect. It can also be used as a discussion between the creator and evaluator.

	Overall Understanding of Subject	Word Choice	Overall Visual Effect
X	This will indicate how well your ideas flow to create a full picture of who you are.	This will indicate whether or not you have met the expectations established for word choice.	This will indicate how well you have put together the visuals, creating a collage of ideas that represent you.
1	Words are disjointed and random. They provide no consistent understanding of the subject.	There are less than 10 words or phrases. Those present do not match the established criteria.	Pieces are either missing entirely or there is a lack of commitment to the visual representation. The message and meaning is unclear.
2	Some words make sense together, while others seem random.	There are 10–15 words or phrases that follow the established criteria.	The message and meaning are starting to become clear, but some aspects are haphazard and do not contribute.
3	There is an overall picture beginning to form, though some words and ideas detract from the overall idea.	There are 15–20 words or phrases that follow the established criteria.	The piece is starting to meet the minimum criteria.

4	Most of the words contribute to the understanding of the subject with few exceptions.	There are 20–25 words or phrases that follow the established criteria.	There is some effort put into the visuals and some higher-level representation to the overall piece. Some aspects contribute to the overall understanding of the subject.
5	There is a complete understanding of the subject. There is a feeling of stepping into the subject's shoes.	There are 25 words or phrases and at least 5 verbs, 5 nouns, and 5 adjectives. They all make sense together as a snapshot.	The overall piece is visually dynamic. There is obvious thought and effort put into the presentation and it adds to the understanding of the subject.
Additional Comments and Suggestions for Improvement			
Pure Praise! This is what I liked the most!			

Please assure your name is clearly indicated.
We want to give credit to the right poet!

Modifications: Poetic Snapshot Poem Activity–Germination

Primary Challenge:

Modification here is as simple as how you word what you want the students to do; it all depends on how aware they are of nouns, verbs, and adjectives. I also make sure I start by offering them other things to describe collectively. For example, I like to bring in animals (class pets, not wild animals) and have the new poets make a collective list of all the words we can possibly use to describe them. It also helps new poets to build both comfort and a repertoire of words to describe something both physically and beyond. Once you've had a chance to build a list with your new poets, it then becomes an organic next step to ask them to make lists about themselves.

Ask guiding questions here as well, like "How would you describe yourself?" "What are some things you love that make you happy?" "What are some things in your life that are important to you?" and "What do you like to do when you're in school / out of school?" You can also just as easily adapt this activity to be a collage, where the students find and cut out words or images that represent them. I've also made sure to complete this activity at the beginning and the end of the school year to show the new poets just how much they've grown and changed as people. It ends up being a neat personal portfolio piece for each of them to use to celebrate their growth after germination.

Upping the Poetic Challenge:

I have challenged new poets to create not only a poetic snapshot on paper but something with movement, depth, and dimension that brings the chosen representations of the self to life in the visual arts. In this additional challenge, I ask the new poets to first choose the words, then turn them into a physical experience. Two of the most memorable to me were a student who created clothing with words woven in and another who took mannequin segments and collaged words and images onto the parts. Exceptional!

Some new poets need a little guidance to share their thoughts and feelings with others, so having a step-by-step system like this is often helpful for those who prefer a more structured process. Some poets need specifics, examples, and hand-holding, while others need freedom and trust. Your relationship with each new poet will help them build and understand their authentic relationship with their voice and how it is used.

Sadie
(Grade 6)

FILL IN THE POEM

Have you ever heard of a slam poem? Have you ever seen slam poetry in action? Let's actually make one happen! Your first job will be to fill in the spaces below as accurately and honestly as you can.

1. Name the animal you feel you are the most like. Not your favorite animal necessarily, but one you feel reflects who you are as a person.

_____

2. Tell me one basic fact about that animal. (You may need to look it up!)

_____

_____

_____

3. Tell me one way you feel you act like this animal.

_____

_____

_____

_____

4. Tell me the most amazingly interesting and fantastic fact you can find about this animal. (Really search for something great!)

_____

_____

_____

_____

5. Tell me your absolute, most important physical personal item.

_____

_____

_____

_____

6. Tell me what it is about this item that makes it important/ special to you.

_____

_____

_____

_____

7. Tell me three of the very best words you think people would use to describe you.

_____

_____

_____

_____

8. Tell me your favorite sound in the world.

_____

_____

_____

_____

9. Tell me one thing you are afraid of.

_____

_____

_____

10. Tell me something you think is incredibly strong.

_____

_____

_____

Use your answers in the slam poetry stanza below to create your own fill-in-the-blank slam poem!

> There are times when my heart tells me I am more (1) than human being. The people who know me may say that because, like this animal, I also (2). But I know it is because I (3) and sometimes I (4) as well. In my chest, caged behind ribs, my heart is like a (5). It beats rhythms that sound like (6). It beats louder and louder, each thump reminding me I am (7), (7), and (7), and that the sound of who I am echoes like (8). But I do not forget that (9) exists. So my heart will be as strong as (10) and keep beating.

You may have to edit the way some things are phrased to make sure it makes grammatical sense and feels perfect to you as the slam poet. As a great example, here are the responses from Ms. Meg, a teacher and librarian from Winnipeg, Manitoba, Canada, that became her final poem!

1. Bear
2. They're super nappers
3. Take care of the cubs
4. Sloth bears have the shaggiest fur!
5. Pictures

6. They're memories
7. Smart, Caring, Teacher
8. Rain or someone saying "I love you"
9. Complete and total isolation
10. Steel

These responses made her beautiful final poem sound like this:

There are times when my heart tells me I am more bear than human being.

The people who know me may say that because, like this animal, I also am a super napper. But I know it is because I take care of my cubs, and sometimes, I have the shaggiest fur as well. In my chest, caged behind ribs, my heart is like a picture. It beats rhythms that sound like memories. It beats louder and louder, each thump reminding me I am smart, caring, and a teacher, and that the sound of who I am echoes like rain or like someone saying "I love you." But I do not forget that complete and total isolation exist. So my heart will be as strong as steel and keep beating.

Now, it's your turn! Don't forget you'll be sharing your slam poem greatness, so be ready to share a little about yourself and the poem of how your heart beats!

Modifications: Fill in the Poem Slam Poetry Activity–Germination

Primary Challenge:

I modify the Fill in the Poem activity for younger slam poets by making the questions and the structured poem a little more simple to respond to and fill out. I usually stick close to the animal behavior questions because those are simple analogy points for slam poets of all ages. People see themselves well in the behaviors of animals. I also give them a chance to build a fill-in-the-blank slam poem based on someone they love and care about. I've used this one with a writing group I worked with in grade three around Mother's Day, and some of the pieces those slam poets created for their mothers made for some very personal gifts.

Upping the Poetic Challenge:

I have the students create their own fill-in-the-blank poems by asking them to "interview" their fellow slam poets and create a poetic gift with the responses. This is also a great way for them to get to know and celebrate their classmates. I've done it with as few as three responses as a warm-up activity, and as many as twenty responses as a biography activity, where students had to fill in slots based on their knowledge of famous historical figures they've researched. I've also had them fill in the blanks from the perspective of characters from novels to get them thinking about their possible experiences. My favorite one was a fill-in-the-blank slam poem from the perspective of Winston Churchill. Brilliant.

This is a true foray into slam poetry. It is simultaneously a deeply personal piece of poetry that allows a new slam poet to tell us how they see themselves and a universal structure they can use to feel safe in sharing with others. It's the beauty of each student wearing the same uniform while bringing their own skills to the team. Some people dunk, some people shoot threes, but you all win a championship under the same banner.

I suggest diving deep into the fun of the slam poetry experience. Because so much of this will be achieved by safely filling in the blanks, I've found that new slam poets feel free to get up and perform rather than simply read it aloud. I share with them a brilliant clip of Tom Hanks on *Late Night with Jimmy Fallon* doing a slam poetry piece about *Full House*. This is also a good moment to remind them about "snaps." Slam poets don't applaud often; we snap our fingers when we see or hear something we love. This little tradition originated in the 1950s, when a generation of beatnik poets wanted to show their appreciation for great work at poetry readings but decided that clapping wasn't a cool enough way to show their support. Ironically, this counterculture way of showing appreciation has now become a cornerstone of slam poetry in the same way Warhol's soup cans became the symbol of what that art form could be. I encourage you to motivate your new slam poets to offer up some heavy snaps after their performances. It's an invitation for both you and your new slam poet community to embrace the vibe of sharing, snapping, and opening yourself to the world as a slam poet.

DREAM LIKE LANGSTON HUGHES

Langston Hughes was an exceptional poet, novelist, playwright, and social activist, among many other things. He is an important figure in the Harlem Renaissance and is credited as the father of jazz poetry, a form of poetry that moved and worked around sounds in the way beautiful jazz music does. Some say this was the early roots of slam poetry.

Hughes was passionate about describing the everyday Black experience in real and meaningful ways. He wanted people who weren't Black to have a taste of the hardest and most wonderful pieces of that experience, and he wanted those who were Black to have more ways to see the beauty in and reasons for celebrating who they are. His work is important and effective and often uses imagery to describe unique experiences in ways that can make them universally appreciated.

Imagery is the use of specific language to bring to mind a picture or concrete sensation of a person, place, thing, or experience. Often, it uses the five senses to connect one person's experience to another's by finding something they both have experienced or can understand. For example, if you have never jumped in a lake, someone who has can help you understand it by saying that it feels as surprisingly cold as the first few freezing seconds when you turn on the shower.

Langston Hughes's poem "Harlem" leans on imagery to explore something very individual (dreams), so we can experience the tastes, sounds, smells, feel, and visuals of what those dreams are when we don't chase them. Read it. Enjoy it. Think about it. And on the next page, list how this poem uses imagery to connect to each of our senses. Think deeply about how this simple piece of writing brings the reader into the experience. How does Langston Hughes use specific language choices to activate the five senses? In the space below, describe how he brilliantly uses imagery.

How does this poem use imagery to connect with your sense of smell?

_____

_____

_____

How does this poem use imagery to connect with your sense of sight?

_____

_____

_____

How does this poem use imagery to connect with your sense of touch?

_____

_____

_____

How does this poem use imagery to connect with your sense of taste?

_____

_____

_____

How does this poem use imagery to connect with your sense of hearing?

_____

_____

_____

Now, it's your turn! Your dreams, why you dream them, and how you see yourself achieving them are unique to you and your perspective. In the space provided below, write your biggest dream for the future in the middle. In each of the five sense sections, think about how you would describe that dream through the five senses. That will be the basis for the poem you'll write!

Now that you've gotten all these great imagery ideas jotted down, put them all together on a separate piece of paper and get ready to *share*, because that's what poets do! (Don't worry, you'll get the supportive snaps of your fellow poets because that's also what poets do!) Share those dreams!

Modifications: Dream Like Langston Hughes Poem Activity–Germination

Primary Challenge:

Modification of this activity for younger new poets may require being less focused on their individual dreams (or it may not; again, you know your team best). I find that with younger new slam poets, it's more effective to give them concrete concepts to approach as a group. I've used prompts like "What does this classroom look/sound/taste/feel/smell like?" so they have something universal to build off of. Then, I move on to something a little more abstract and personal, like "What does your family look/sound/taste/feel/smell like?" However you want to present it is up to you. I've also seen a tremendous variety of methods to catalog, present, and celebrate these little new poet perspectives. Be creative!

Upping the Poetic Challenge:

I've modified this activity for older new slam poets by having them go through the development of their Dream Like Langston Hughes poem, then take the rest of the night to write a full-on experience they can share with their fellow poets the next day. I challenge them to bring in something that smells, looks, tastes, sounds, and feels like their dream. Then, their method of presentation is to take the other slam poets through those sensational experiences and bring them into their dream as thoroughly as possible. It takes the onus off of the writing and puts the focus more on presentation and representation. When we talk about culminating activities at the end of the book, I'll give you a few ideas on how to guide exceptionally shy poets out of their shells when it comes to performance-based poetry.

PHOTOBOMB POETRY

In the digital age, we are a people who like to take pictures, whether it's selfies, family pictures, pictures of our food, overly artsy pictures, or nature shots. We are lucky that we get to catalog all of these great moments, and this activity gives us the chance to share the experiences captured in those photos!

STEP 1: PICK A PIC

We all scroll through our photos from time to time, but this time, there's a purpose! Decide on criteria as a group and find a photo either on your phone or (time permitting) at home. You might decide on general criteria, like "find a picture that reminds you of a great story," "find a picture that features someone you love," or "find a picture that makes you smile/laugh." You could also decide on specific and challenging criteria, like "find a picture that has the color red in it" or "find a picture taken someplace other than at home or in school." Make sure the photo is classroom appropriate and can be shared because that is, after all, the end goal.

STEP 2: NOTE YOUR NOTES

Your job here as a poet is to bring your audience into the experience of that photo. It's important in this step to ask yourself some important questions and jot down notes so you have lots of information to build your poem off of.

- What is your emotional intention? How do you want the audience to feel when they hear your poem about this picture?
- What kind of words/ideas will you want to include in your poem to make sure they feel that way?
- How are you going to make sure your audience *feels* what you felt in that moment? You want to make sure your poem feels like something they can dive into and experience for themselves. This is a good place to focus on the five senses.
- What would the people and things in that photo want you to say about them? Even if they're nonliving things, think about what they'd want expressed so others can enjoy the moment captured in the photo!

STEP 3: DRAFT IT UP

Draft a poem that will take your audience inside the moment of that photo.

STEP 4: MAKE IT BETTER

Editing and evolving a poem is always important. Seek feedback, practice out loud, and ask yourself how you can make your poem even more magical.

STEP 5: SLAM THAT PHOTOBOMB POEM

Time to hit the audience with that hot fire poem action and bring them into the captured moment.

STEP 6: SNAPS AND SNAP BACKS

Soak in the awesome support and snaps from the other new poets in the room and be ready to give them that same support and positive energy.

Modifications: Photobomb Poetry
Poem Activity–Germination

Primary Challenge:

To modify, I ask poets to bring in a photo from home, then we talk through their feelings in the moments depicted in the pictures. What's even more fun is having the new poets draw a particular moment they remember in their lives. Then, I give them space to share their feelings about that moment with the group, focusing on their five senses.

Upping the Poetic Challenge:

For those who need more of a challenge, I instruct them to go out into the world and complete this activity again with random criteria given by another person for their photos. For example, they might ask a friend for a number, then go back to that photo in their phone's photo album and write a timed (usually five minutes) slam poem about being in the moment of that photo. These criteria challenge the new poets to complete the activity in a set period of time while also giving them the advantage of working from their own experience.

This activity was actually born through my work with educators. I wanted to find ways for educators to express the power of poetry to their students as a means of building voice and connection, rather than just telling them how much it would mean for them. I've had educators take out their phones, select criteria, then write and be with their poem for a few minutes. Then, they'd go around the room introducing themselves to other brand-new poets through those photos. It was so positive that I started to use this approach with students.

In one of my sessions, an educator shied away from sharing because she worried her slam poem "wasn't good." That's the thing about personal experiences and poems: your poem will never be "good" or "bad." It's *your* truth either way; that's what makes it so dang important!

I like that you're so kind to me and you helped me learn to bike. I like that you taught me how to turn like four different ways on my bike. We got to bike on the street on our bike date and bike back down the street back home. Being on that bike date made me feel like we were the only best two bikers.

Sawyer (Kindergarten)

PAINT SWATCH POETRY

There has always been an association between colors and feelings. Different colors make us feel warm and happy, while others bring out passion and a connection to different places and times. Visual artists have been taking advantage of these color tricks for a long time, and now, it's time for us poets to take a crack at it!

STEP 1

You'll be randomly given paint swatches, the color samples paint companies provide so you can see what colors might make your new kitchen sparkle.

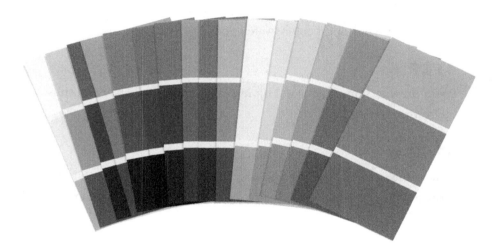

STEP 2

Take a look at the swatches and write down what the colors make you think and how they make you feel. Pour out all the words, ideas, and thoughts that come to mind when you see and feel those colors. There are no wrong answers; the more you put on the page, the more you'll have to work with later! You could even think about the names the colors are given. Whatever inspires you, write it down!

STEP 3

Your challenge now is a big one, so you'll really have to use all your poet muscles on it! Take your swatches and write a mini poem for each color. You can write a haiku if you'd like, or you could write your own version of a short poem. Whatever you decide, make sure you write one for each of the shades. Can you make it more intense as the colors get more intense? Can you make the first one feel light while making the others deeper and more interesting as they get darker? You're an awesome poet, so of course you can!

STEP 4

As always, great poets edit and rework, always striving to share the very best version of their work! Take a minute to edit, read your poem aloud, seek feedback, or whatever else you need to do to make sure you're putting together your finest color swatch poem!

STEP 5

Poem presentation time! Stand up in front of your audience and show them what you've got!

STEP 6

Soak in the awesome support and snaps from the other new poets in the room and be ready to give them that same support and positive energy.

Modifications: Paint Swatch Poetry Activity–Germination

Primary Challenge:

Even though this activity is designed with younger new poets in mind, I often use the physical aspects of this modification when I work with older new poets. What I like to do is make rainbow walls, with each section of the wall representing a different color. The little new poets to look at each of the colors and imagine how they feel and what comes to mind in each section. I then ask them to write a few words on pieces of paper and pin them onto the wall in the sections they are inspired by. Afterward, we go over the words and talk about why those words came to mind and what made them feel the way they did. We talk about what it felt like to write a big wall poem rainbow together as a team. I've also extended the fun with little new poets by doing a different color every day and diving deep into the feelings, ideas, and images of each, which usually results in a really exceptional rainbow poem.

Upping the Poetic Challenge:

Being a big art fan, both fridge-door art and famous works, I like to upgrade this to an art study. I show students some phenomenal works of art, and we talk about the work the colors are doing to bring major emotions forward and tell a story. I then like to divide the poets into smaller groups and give them their own works of art to consider so they can build ideas about the colors and feelings of that piece of art, branching off at the end to write their own poetry pieces and present their work of art as a backdrop. There are a lot of ways to structure this activity, but the idea is that the new poets will really focus on the colors, emotional intention, and language of feelings behind the artwork that links our experiences and understanding as human beings.

This activity requires you to go to a hardware store. I'm sorry if you're anything like me and that means you'll be walking out with not only what you need but a pile of home improvement supplies and a list of plans a mile long. What I like about this activity is that it provides another layer for new poets to consider when they think about the emotional intention and impact of their poetry. Color, tone, mood, and sound all play into what an audience experiences through good poetry.

This is the badge I use for new slam poets who complete the germination phase. Feel free to copy and use this one, make your own, or have a new slam poet design one for you!

CHAPTER 3
GROWTH TO FLOWERING PLANT

"I DON'T EVEN KNOW WHAT TO CALL MYSELF."

I've always worked on the assumption that everyone has this incredible life poem inside of them that they've been writing in the lining of their muscles, bones, memories, and every little experience they've had. I still absolutely live by that; every person I have the privilege of interacting with is another person whose poem I feel driven to hear. I feel it is the most beautiful responsibility of my life to hear, amplify, and share those poems.

For so much of my time working to grow the voices of others, I believed the only thing those new poets needed was someone to listen, someone to show them that their poem had value. I felt like it would flow out of them and into the world like a dam with a hole in it. I thought it was as easy as access and opportunity. I was wrong. I can trace back to a singular moment where I saw and embraced the metaphor that new poets were actually like seeds that needed more from their environment, rather than simple dams straining under the pressure of what they were ready to share with the world.

I was working with a group of high school students in a two-day workshop. We had spent the first morning nurturing those who expressed that they didn't often feel valued or heard for their individual stories and voices, and they seemed to be germinating tremendously. They were seeing themselves as poets with important truths to share. I had done dozens of workshops with hundreds of students at that point, and it always felt good to go in and encourage new poets. I felt like I knew what I was doing. There were some who were reluctant, but I felt they just needed to feel safe and valued before they shared with us. I'd developed ways to make that happen and felt confident I could germinate even the seeds with the toughest shells.

There was a young gentleman who seemed to be one of those reluctant new poets. I usually saw kids like him with almost empty pages and knew from experience that I'd have to show them they're safe and valued before they would open up. No behavior is without motivation. This young gentleman happened to have the long black hair of his First Nations heritage braided down his back, with a beaded jean jacket that proudly showcased the symbols of his clan across his shoulders and back. He had friends around him who were also First Nations who were embracing the writing and the chance to speak in welcoming spaces. He had support and examples and as much comfort as our community could provide. But this exceptional young man taught me a lesson I had to learn.

He wore the body language of frustration, and his face twisted often when it was time to write. He had crumpled pages, breathed out in loud huffs, and was tapping his feet and pencil in constant rhythm. I walked over to work with him, assuming I'd be coming over to the typical blank pages these reluctant students usually exhibit. But this young man, this passionate and capable young man, had page after page of writing. He had drawings, edits, question marks, and ideas, and it was good. I was dumbfounded. I had no idea what I could offer a new poet who clearly had this much to say and was surrounded by all the best community pieces a new poet could have. So I asked him, "Bud, what do you need here? Because it looks like you have the words, so what's missing?" His answer taught me a lot.

"I don't even know what to call myself," he responded.

I didn't have time to be confused before he started to shuffle through filled pages listing off all of the things he had written down in self-reference.

"I've got a dozen damn pages, and I've called myself a dozen damn things. You tell us to speak our truth, but am I a Native? Am I First Nations? Am I Anishinaabe? Cree? Sports call me Redskin and Chief, despite the racism of that, sometimes they say Indian, even though I know that all came from a mistake where colonizers thought this was India. Peter Pan called me Red Man. I've got textbooks that have called me Indigenous and others call me savage and Amerindian. How am I supposed to speak my truth and put my poem out there if me and everyone hearing it won't even recognize me in it? How is this my story when I don't know how to make people recognize me?"

Admittedly, the question floored me. I had no idea how to respond to something so big, something I hadn't heard from a new poet before. Then, a lightbulb went off in my head. I could connect with this new poet through my own story. I mean, that's what this is all about anyway! So I looked sagely at him and offered this nugget of who I am:

"Listen, my friend. I hear you. I've recently found out that I'm Métis, and I've been trying to figure out what that means to my story." It seemed like a great idea until he replied with, "Dammit! My dad is white and my mom is Indigenous. Does that mean I have to think about whether that's part of who I am to people too?! C'mon!"

Thank goodness other students exist because one of his friends stepped forward and changed the direction of a rapidly downhill-moving moment. With a hand on her frustrated fellow new poet's shoulder, she offered, "Listen, I don't think it matters what other people want to call you. Personally, I've always just seen you as the boy who loves his kookum, and that makes him proud of his family name. You don't owe anyone anything; you just owe it to yourself to love the story you're telling about yourself and feel like it's your truth. Right, Mr. Johnston? Isn't that what you've been telling us?"

Of course I wanted to take full credit for such incredible insight, but I had to give it to her. "No," I answered, "what you've just said is so much better a version of what I'm trying to tell you. Thanks."

The young man's demeanor melted and a smile spread like wildfire across his face. See, "kookum" means grandmother, and she was right: he loved his. He spent the rest of the day writing and talking with a relaxed and positive body language, but he still did not want to share anything formally. He kept telling me, "Ask me tomorrow," with a knowing smile. On the second day of our workshop, he came in early with bins full of bannock (fried bread) and jam that he had spent the previous night making with his kookum. He shared with everyone. It was the best bannock I have eaten to this day, and I love bannock. Then, he hit us with a poem he'd finished the night before while cooking. He introduced his piece as "What My Kookum Calls Me." It was incredible.

I learned that it is infinitely more powerful to be open to hearing how a new slam poet sees themselves and their story than to believe you know the best ways to help them speak. I also learned that listening wasn't enough, that being honestly open to the truth of another meant asking, adjusting, relistening, double-checking, and letting them see your desire to help them speak their absolute truth because it matters that it is heard on its own terms.

It is infinitely more powerful to be open to hearing how a new slam poet sees themselves and their story than to believe you know the best ways to help them speak.

Here again, I'm thankful that the way I see poets evolving together is echoed so well through the life cycle of plants. The seed is the idea and the spark. The germination is finding that little sprout of poetry that breaks seed to protect and build on, that view and understanding of the self that is worth pursuing further. The process from germination to flowering plant is about just that: growth after breaking through. This is where the classroom seems more like a garden. Just like diverse plants in a garden, all kinds of students need all kinds of unique support to help them grow and flower. That was the other part of the lesson: that the individual and the community are one and the same. They need each other to exist by definition. They need each other to grow into their potential. It's why I believe in the power and magic of poetry for students; it is a group therapy session where the common theme is the individual rather than something external that binds them.

How does my story link to your story and to the activities in this chapter? This young man taught me that a poet needs more than opportunities to tell their story. A poet needs a person to listen to the needs of their process and truth, and that is what the next wave of activities offers. I am hoping to give you ways to take the germinated seeds from the last chapter and give them opportunities to grow and flower within themselves, while meeting their completely unique needs within your larger community.

A poet needs more than opportunities to tell their story. A poet needs a person to listen to the needs of their process and truth, and that is what the next wave of activities offers.

SLAM POET ACTIVITY: FROM GROWTH TO FLOWERING PLANT (EDUCATOR SUPPORT)

STEP 1

Reflect. Taking time to celebrate the pieces you feel help your new poets grow, as well as embracing the beautiful missteps you make, is important for you and the next steps. Make sure you feel good about the way in which you've germinated new slam poets. If you need more time or more activities, then take what you need. The next step should feel like a next step, so make sure you move forward when you feel it is right.

Remember, nobody is ever going to read this unless you show them. There is no better learning than making a mistake or having something not work and evolving through that as an educator. So have at it and be honest. What didn't work? What would you have done differently? What are you going to fail forward from?

Now, flip that coin and spill out the strong points so you can build on them. What did you do right? How did you absolutely rock the last chapter? How did you help new slam poets germinate?

STEP 2

Make a plan for the next steps! It's strategy time!

I'd like to talk about the acronym of P.O.E. Tree, specifically, as part of the plan you're making. Different plants need different things, yes, but the one thing they will universally need is *you*. You will be asked to be the gardener sometimes, and other times, you will be the sun or the rain. Sometimes you'll be asked to be the soil itself, just so new poets have something to hang onto and grow roots from. Whatever you are to each of your individual new poets, make sure you are asking yourself if this is P.O.E.Tree, because this is the time when new poets will need that the most. Your care and support from your handmade vibe and community will allow them to bloom. This is the time to figure out how each of them can grow strong stems and flowers.

P—**Pericardial:** While success in the last chapter looked like a murmuration, success here will look like a garden growing strong. While the last chapter focused on showing your students that you really care about their poetry, making sure they felt safe exposing those layers closest to their hearts, this chapter is asking you to put their stories close to your own heart. This is also how you grow from an individual's voice to a community blooming together and supporting one another.

How are you making each new poet's truth pericardial to you? How are you making sure that they know their individual stories are important to you? How are you going to start building a community by having them place each other's voices close to their hearts?

I will. . .

O—**Open:** The last chapter asked you to be open to seeing your students as they were asking to be seen. Once they know you're open to their stories as they want them to be heard, it becomes your responsibility to meaningfully support their voices and processes as they figure out how to go from seeing themselves inside their hearts and minds to expressing themselves *outside* through their pens and voices.

How will you make sure to hear their version of who they are? How will you help them bring their poems from inside their heart to the outside world without putting too much of your influence on it? How will you help them be open to one another's truths as they evolve into a true community?

I will. . .

E—**Electrifying:** In this chapter, electrifying is about making sure your new slam poets have the energy and motivation to keep working, trying, and editing until they see themselves truthfully in their work.

How are you going to make sure your new poets feel motivated enough to cross that finish line with a valuable end product? How will you make sure they are genuinely electrified about what their fellow poets have to say?

I will. . .

T—**Tree:** In the last chapter, I asked how you would avoid making this a one-off poetry lesson. In this chapter, I want to make sure that even as you help each new poet grow and flower, they understand that this all means something, that every poem and poet is a part of something bigger than themselves.

How will you make sure each new poet balances the individual importance of their truth with the growth of the community that surrounds and supports them? How will you show them that community is valuable and is the intention behind these next steps?

I will. . .

GROWTH TO FLOWERING PLANT

Things I want to remember when mapping this out (Notes to Self):

_____

_____

_____

Remember, you don't have to have all the answers right away; this is just to get you thinking honestly about where you're at. Give yourself that grace.

STEP 3

Consider the concepts of collaborative storytelling and emotional mindfulness through another plant metaphor. Fireweed is a striking and resilient plant that grows in northern parts of Canada and in Alaska. I first saw this beautiful plant when I was on a road trip, discovering the Great White North in Whitehorse and Skagway. These areas are prone to seasonal wildfires that burn off the old growth and make way for something new. Fireweed is always the first thing that grows back after the fire. I think about that little plant and the power of growth through ashes when I consider how important collaborative storytelling and emotional mindfulness are here. I think about what it takes to break through and be seen bright and new against the ash of what used to be. I think about all that it takes from the surrounding environment to make it possible for that new plant to germinate and reach out for growth. I think about how incredible it was to drive along these perilous highways and see that pop of pink against the black, reminded more and more that, often, to believe in themselves, new poets and people in general have to grow through burned-down versions of themselves.

Collaborative Storytelling

In the previous chapter, collaborative storytelling looked like you providing emotional support and value to each new poet's story. Your part in the collaboration was the idea that, at times, they would need you to be the echo of validation and structure for the poetry they were creating. The intention of this chapter on growth and flowering is for you to take on a more varied role as a collaborative storyteller with each new poet. Your job here is to think about how you're helping them each write their own poems within their own truths in a way that others can effectively interact with while also making them active and caring members of a developing slam poet community. You are the environment that will allow those little fireweeds to push through the ash. People driving by tend to say, "Wow, those are beautiful flowers," and not so much "Wow, that must be a really incredible environment for germination and growth that allows those beautiful flowers to be seen," but that's the beauty of your role. If you are an effective collaborative storyteller, their bloom will be more celebrated than the environment you provide.

Emotional Mindfulness

I love Rita Pierson. Not only was she a lifelong and renowned educator, she was a talented and thoughtful storyteller. A staunch advocate for students before her passing, she gave an important TED talk in which she spoke to why she believed each one should have a champion. I agree with her. She also said that students don't learn from people they don't like. I agree with her there, too, but I think students don't like people they don't know. Mathematically, that means they don't learn from people they don't know. That can include themselves sometimes. Taking the time to get to know yourself is a real privilege for most.

That's one of the most meaningful things poetry offers students: it helps them know themselves so they can learn through themselves. Emotional mindfulness in this step requires you to be aware of the impact self-learning and presentation can have. New poets will be diving into deep pieces of themselves and getting to know themselves, and it will be up to you to make sure they have the support they need to learn and present effectively. You're the emotional safety net for both the new poets in discovery and those around them who are hearing those new perspectives and truths.

STEP 4

Buffet time!

These chapter activities are designed to be individually meaningful while providing opportunities to bring students together as a collective and a community. Make your plan, go through this tasty buffet section, and pick and choose what is going to work best for you. Use them all, use a few, vary the levels of use, modify, and adapt. Frankenstein this smorgasbord! Make the pieces of what I've given you into the right kind of monster, for not only your new poets but their evolution into a slam poetry community. How much time are you dedicating to it? What is your end goal? What does a successful slam poet community look like for your new poets? How do you want them to celebrate themselves while embracing something bigger than they could ever be alone? Answer these questions then grow and flower. Take time to dive into the deep end of these activities. Finally, share, celebrate, and help your students bloom together into an incredible poet community. Garden away!

Welcome back to the buffet! Time for another helping! Let's dirty up a stack of plates! With this being the growth and flowering chapter, all of the following activities are designed to push your students to learn about themselves and develop the connections and skills to create a community. Now that they're germinated as new poets, how will you help them grow and flower? What do you feel this community and its connections need to look like? Remember, pick and choose, modify and mold, until you have something that fits your team.

BUFFET BREAKDOWN
(ANOTHER OFFERING OF DELICIOUS ACTIVITIES)

1. **What Do We Love?**—This activity is one that helps not only with self-perspective but embracing the collective "we" spirit.

2. **Dada Poem**—This is a collective piece where new poets get to appreciate the perspectives of others while embracing chance, creating beauty, and having a little fun outside of formal structure.

3. **Slam It into the Void**—This activity is about expressing feelings in a safe space while being respected and supported.

4. **Haiku for Heart**—This activity challenges new slam poets to take a big experience and process and present it through the much smaller and more structured format of the traditional haiku.

5. **Get a Sense of Me**—This activity invites new poets to think about themselves abstractly and opens them up to using their five senses to share unique experiences with others.

6. **What Was Your First Poem?**—This activity is about figuring out how each individual expresses their story. They'll take a look back at their own life and try to write a poem about the first poem they ever wrote, before they had the words to do so.

7. **A Love Poem to Yourself / Thing That You Love**—This activity is about celebrating the parts of ourselves we should love and be thankful for. It's also a chance to personify and thank the things that make each of us who we are.

WHAT DO WE LOVE?

Poetry is a challenge because you have to think about how you're going to use your voice to connect others with your experiences and feelings. This will be a poem written and presented by all of us, so it will be all of our individual voices talking about the things we love, but we'll embrace all of it as a team!

Instructions

1. You'll each get a grid paper with spaces to write things you love. When you get the paper, it will be your responsibility to fill in your "The Answer" as honestly as possible (with classroom-appropriate answers). Please only fill in one at a time, then be ready to pass it!

2. You'll pass the paper to another slam poet in the room so they can fill in the next "The Answer" section and contribute to the poem! But remember, please only fill in one at a time, then get ready to pass it again!

3. You'll pass it again and fill in the next section. You'll keep filling in one section and passing it on until all the sections are full. The completed form that ends up in front of you will be the one you work with!

4. Take a minute to read over the answers. In the third column (the one labeled "The Feels"), write down a single word that expresses how you'd want to speak each answer. Do you feel like you should say it happily? Angrily? Should you read it loudly or quietly? What is the one word that comes to mind when you envision yourself speaking it? We're preparing to present here!

5. Whoever is leading the activity will decide on the order of presenters. It can be any order that works for your team and gives everyone a chance to present. This might look like standing in a circle, reading things in order, or picking and choosing a few of the ones that really stand out to you. It might look like each

poet reading a few, then passing it to someone else. Decide how it works best for your group!

6. It's also important to decide on a format for presentation. For example, you might decide that each spoken sentence could start with "We are a class who loves. . ." or "We are a room full of people who love. . ." or "In this space, we love. . ."

7. Present your poem together, for each other, with each other, and as a team!

THE POET GRID OF LOVE

The Question	The Answer	The Feels (How will you express the answer you're reading?)
What is something you love to do outside of school?		
What is something you love to eat?		
What is a sound you love?		
What is a smell you love?		
What is something you love to do with friends?		
What is something you love to imagine yourself doing in the future?		
What is the name of a living thing (or a few living things) you love?		

What is a place you love to go to?		
What is a physical thing (an item) you love?		

Now that you've filled in the grid answer by answer, remember that it is time to think about "the Feels." How are you going to use your important and awesome voice to express the pieces others have provided for you?

Now, it's time for a team piece poem! Go in, poets!

Below, you'll find a grid that was completed by a grade four new poet.

The Question	The Answer	The Feels (How will you express the answer you're reading?)
What is something you love to do outside of school?	Play video games	With my face scrunched up like I'm playing hard and with my thumbs moving around like I'm really into the game.
What is something you love to eat?	Ice cream	I should hold my hand up like I have a cone and pretend to take big licks. If I have a big happy look on my face and really move my neck, people will know I like it a lot.
What is a sound you love?	Waves from the lake	I want people to know I feel really calm, so I'm going to close my eyes and smile and breathe in deeply when I say it.

What is a smell you love?	Oven cookies	I should get an excited look on my face and rub my belly like I'm looking into the oven window all excited.
What is something you love to do with friends?	Play at recess	Oh! I should move around the room when I say it, like "I. . .like. . .to. . .play . . .tag. . .with. . .my . . .friends!"
What is something you love to imagine yourself doing in the future?	Being a singer on a stage	I think I should sing this one while I say it so people know I really love being onstage and feel good up there.
What is the name of a living thing (or a few living things) you love?	Walter, Wessex, Weasley, and Chilkoot (our cats)	I should move around like a cat so they know how I feel watching the cats move.
What is a place you love?	Disneyland!	Ooh! I should answer like I'm on a rollercoaster so they know how much fun I imagine myself having!
What is a physi-cal thing (an item) you love?	I have a few books I really love.	I should say it with my hands in front of my face so they all know I really love being deep into my books.

Modifications: What Do We Love? Collective Poem Activity—Growth to Flowering Plant

Primary Challenge:

This activity lends well to little new poets. All it takes is really clear instructions with slightly modified language. I've used this activity with many little new slam poets. I find it helps them when the person in charge writes the words down on large paper or the board as they're going. It's a good excuse to think about some of the writing outcomes as well.

Upping the Poetic Challenge:

To create a challenge, I tend to scrap the grid part itself and treat it more like an interview. The new poets still use the same questions, but they go around the room and actively engage with one another, asking questions, listening to the why of each answer, taking some notes, then building a full poem based on the love they've discovered in the room. When it comes to the presentation aspect of this, each new poet tends to speak the entire poem of the love they discovered in their interactions around the room.

In this activity, they get to speak their truth in safe ways by writing down what they love, but they know they'll have to entrust the other members of their team in the room. I use this activity often when working with competitive slam poetry teams because it instantly develops community connection and safety. I have also done this with entire staff groupings of educators, which builds quick connections between people as they hear what they love from the mouths of others.

DADA POEM

THIS IS NOT A HANDOUT! (YES, BUT IS IT ART?)

For this activity, having no handout and less structure is part of the fun of the writing experience. Dada poems are based on an art movement (Dadaism) that was characterized by two things: 1) opposition to reason and 2) embracing chance and accident as ways to create opportunities for beauty. I am going to detail a few methods of creating Dada poems with your learners, all of which embrace creating something beautiful together as a community of poets by forgoing the structure of traditional writing activities.

All you need to do is choose one of the methods, do the minimal setup required for each, and take a chance!

METHOD ONE: EXPERIENCE CIRCLE

In method one, you'll prepare by selecting as many photos or pieces of artwork as you have students. Print them and tape them on the walls in a circle. Place a new poet in front of each piece of artwork, with something to write on and something to write with. Tell them this will be about reaction and immediate feeling, so they shouldn't overthink it! (Setting a time limit can help.)

Once they look at the first work of art, instruct them to write down the very first (classroom-appropriate) word that comes to mind. There are no wrong answers! Once finished, each new poet will move clockwise to the next piece of art and repeat the process of writing down the first word that comes to mind. Repeat the process until each student has a single word inspired by each piece of art.

Once they've had a chance to write a word for each, each individual will turn into the center of the circle and read their new poetry creation! I usually give them a few minutes to read them over and think about how they want to read their Dada poems; this allows them to feel comfortable and ready to dive into being an expressive poet!

METHOD TWO: EXPERIENCE CIRCLE–TEAMS

This method is similar to the first one, only it allows new poets to work in small groups. Again, you'll print out works of art and place them in a few different spots. (I should also mention that going to an art gallery is an amazing option for methods one and two, if at all possible. Even the presentation can happen at the gallery; just choose a space for your group and set them up to create art beside art!) You'll divide your new poets using whatever method you prefer and assign them to a work of art. Within a given time frame, ask them to write a specific amount of words (say, five to ten) that come to mind when they look at their assigned piece of art.

After time has elapsed, have the new poets stand in a line facing the rest of the community. I have one of them hold the piece of art up, or, if your technology allows, you can project a larger version onto the wall so everyone can experience the piece. Then, in order, each student will read one single word. Then you'll rotate back through, with each poet offering another word in what is now a collective Dada poem. That way, there will be a loop of single words offered by each poet that creates the poem itself. You'll keep going until they're out of words, and you'll have presented (or spit, as us slam poets say) a team Dada poem!

METHOD THREE: TEAM WORD COLLAGE

The next option is based on random wordplay. If you want to give your new poets a chance to write, they can just write poetry on their own. This can take on whatever form you want, but please make them aware from the beginning that they'll be cutting it up! You can also distribute old magazines and have students cut out the random and wonderful words they find.

If you have tables, you could have each table accumulate a box of words cut into pieces. They'll then trade their boxes (or envelopes or whatever you're keeping your word clippings in) and take a word or two (depending on the number you've decided on ahead of time) and place those words on a sheet of paper (they can tape them, glue them, recopy them, or whatever you decide for your team!). You'll pass the boxes or envelopes around in whatever system you've decided on until you've met your word-count goal. In this method, those words serve as a menu to choose from and add to for the creation of their poems. This allows for both interaction with others and the individual freedom to create. Then, you'll give them a few minutes to decide how they'll want to present their Dada poem:

- How does it feel and sound to them?
- What parts do they want to emphasize for their audience?
- What do they think would make their slam poem performance great, even with random words? (Think about what we say beyond the words when we speak.)

Perform, but make sure you set the expectation that after each new poet spits their Dada poem, the audience of listeners will explode with support. That's what poets do.

METHOD FOUR–ROOM OF RANDOMIZATION

Room of Randomization revolves around movement and searching within the physical space of the room. Choose a method that works for your team and have them move toward random words in the room. For example, each new slam poet could make a paper airplane, or you could give each a piece of salt dough and have them throw it around the room (safely!). This will be their "follow object." Once they throw it, they will seek out whichever random word is physically closest to it. For example, if it lands beside a mug, they'll choose the first word they read off that mug, then throw their follow object again. If it then lands close to another poet, they could choose a word on that person's shirt. Whatever is physically closest to their item will determine how they embrace randomization. Then, following the presentation suggestions in method three, they can present their poem!

Modifications: Dada Poem Activity–Growth to Flowering Plant

Primary Challenge:

I modify this activity by showing the entire group one piece of art and instructing them to come up with one word that represents what they see in that piece of art. I then have them "hold the word" in their hearts, hands, or minds, and we go around in a circle while each new poet says their word. I write those words down, then I read the resulting Dadaist poem to them and say, "Wow, look at this amazing poem we all just wrote together!" I then repeat the process with another piece of art, but this time, I instruct them to think more about *how* they're going to say their word with their bodies. Is it a happy word? A silly word? A colorful or movement-based word? I've also used this as a poetry memory game, where they memorize words in a particular sequence and see just how far they can get into the poem by memory.

Upping the Poetic Challenge:

To create a tougher challenge, I introduce them to the concept of a "team piece." A team piece is when a group of poets gets together and develops a piece together to be performed as a collective with all voices involved. I challenge the groups of new poets to take something random and, together, make it into something truly epic in terms of team-built poetry. It is important that each poet contributes and presents orally together.

I wanted this chapter's focus to be about strengthening the individual voice while also creating community. The Dada poem activity is perfect for that because it allows for safe content through randomization, but it gives the poets a chance to think about the *how* of presentation and spoken word.

INTO THE VOID

A void, by definition, is a completely empty space, a place where nothing exists. Today, we're going to send some feelings into the void, where they will disappear forever! It's not always easy to feel certain things. Sometimes you feel things that are heavy and weigh you down. Sometimes things feel frustrating, confusing, or irritating. Sometimes you feel things that are so positive you could burst.

You're allowed to feel anything your heart desires. It is hard to share sometimes. But poetry is all about opening yourself up and connecting to the feelings and experiences of those around you, so we're going to create a poetry space where you can get some things off your chest! Here is the rundown:

1. There will be a bin, box, or bucket at the front or in the middle of the room. That is . . . *the Void*! That is where your poem will rest once you've gotten it off your chest!
2. Find a spot to write. The space should be yours; this isn't a team activity. This is a space for you and your big feels.
3. Choose something specific that you feel strongly about. Again, this can be any feelings on any topic, as long as you can dive deep into those feelings while you're writing.
4. Write. You should challenge yourself to write for the entire time. Write as though getting all the feelings out on the page will help you feel lighter and breathe easier. Write in poems, full sentences, notes, or single words. Put everything you are feeling onto the page. Nobody will read this page but you, so put everything you need to get out onto the page.
5. Once the time is up, you'll have a chance to look at what you've written and prepare yourself to share, but you don't have to worry about putting too many of your feels out there if you don't feel good about it. On a separate piece of paper, you're going to transfer your ideas. Look at everything you wrote and choose what you're going to share out loud. You can rewrite it

as a poem, copy a few main sentences or ideas, or if you're really not ready to do too much sharing, choose at least seven words. They can be any seven words on the page (as long as they're classroom appropriate), but you'll get to go up, say those seven words, and it will feel like you're reading from that big page.

6. You'll present your poem, no matter what it looks like. Everyone will support you when you're done, no matter what.

7. You're already close to the Void, so when you are done, crumple, rip, or nicely deposit your poem into the Void! Don't worry, the person in charge will dispose of them all secretly, so there's no danger!

8. Feel lighter. Embrace slamming into the Void and letting go.

Again, with this chapter, I've put together activities I have used to build a sense of community and safety around individual expression.

Modifications: Slam into the Void Poem Activity—Growth to Flowering Plant

Primary Challenge:

With this activity focused on both talking about and dealing with our feelings, as well as how to be a positive and supportive member of a group, I often use this particular modification for both younger and older new poets. I have the little new poets sit together, and I tell them that we're going to write a poem about a particular feeling. I will say, "We're going to write a poem together about feeling happy! Think for a minute. What does it feel like to be happy? How does your body and your heart know you are happy? I'm going to let you think, then you can each give me up to three words or ideas that let me know how you feel when you are happy. And remember, you can't use the word happy; that's too easy!"

Once they've had a minute to think, I let them know that no matter what words someone else chooses (as long as they are classroom appropriate), we are going to clap or snap for them because we want to show them that however they feel is OK! Then, we go around the circle, the little new poets offer their words, and we clap and snap for each one as a community. Don't forget to offer your words too; you're always an important part of them seeing poem-building and community in action. I then repeat the process with other feelings like anger, frustration, silliness, etc.

Upping the Poetic Challenge:

To level up, I go to some real heavy hitters in the slam poetry game. I show the new slam poets a poem called "Explaining My Depression to My Mother" by Sabrina Benaim. Sabrina is an exceptional Canadian slam poet (and national team champion) who has used her poetry to tell the story of her mental health and the power around being able to name and talk about issues like depression and relationships through slam poetry. I use that piece to show the new poets in the room what happens when you know people will actually listen to your feelings: you start to open up and speak your truth. This always gives me a chance to talk about the responsibility and privilege of community.

Then I show them a poem by Neil Hilborn called "OCD." Neil explains what it's like to be in love and in a relationship with someone when you are living with OCD. Both pieces are not only exceptional slam poems, but they show that putting yourself out there reveals your truth and strength and allows you to be a part of this larger community of people who need you just as much as you need them when it comes to that truth being heard and acknowledged.

Next, I run the same activity with them as in the handout, but I challenge them to organize whatever feelings they have then put them down into a real and meaningful slam poem. Before they share, I sit with the group and ask, "What does this community need to be when others are presenting? What can we do to be there for each other while we're sharing these truths?" I also ask, "What do you need from this group of slam poets around you?" Here, slam poetry is a tool that lends itself well to the intention of this activity.

HAIKU FOR HEART

Life is full of so much that it can often be difficult to process big moments, thoughts, ideas, and experiences. What we feel and how we experience life is what makes us all unique. How we decide to share these feelings and experiences with others is what makes us *poets*!

Your task is straightforward, but it won't be easy. Please follow the instructions below:

STEP 1

Choose an experience or moment in your life that is specific. Maybe it was a trip or a special event or holiday. Think concerts, birthdays, vacations, quarantine, parties, Christmas morning, family reunions, anything that is specific and that you feel you remember well. It doesn't have to be positive; it just has to be a moment that you remember the feeling of distinctly.

STEP 2

Think about the experience. Think about how you would tell someone about that experience so they can understand how it felt. If you're talking about a trip to Disneyland, your audience should know what it feels like to be there after you explain it. (You may choose several moments if you have time during the challenge!)

STEP 3

Turn it into a haiku! A haiku is a challenge. It is a very specific form of language and expression that involves syllables. It always follows the same pattern, 5–7–5.

To help you out with this big task, you will be allowed *two* haikus about the same moment to try and get your experience across to your audience. Really think about your word choice. Each syllable counts here, so make some solid choices! Here are some examples, one based on a positive experience; the other, less than positive:

Disneyland	Quarantine
The smell of churros	My house feels like jail
Coasters, shows, and characters	The inmates are my family
Constant smiling kids	And time moves so slow
This was Disney's dream	I know this is right
A place for magic and hope	I do my part for the team
And fireworks boom	While I miss them too

STEP 4

Present! Poetry is all about connecting through presentation, so make sure you're ready to present the haikus. Good luck! You got this, poet!

This activity is a personal favorite. I personally use it often in my daily life. When things get too big for me or when my thoughts won't calm down enough at night to let me sleep, I take whatever it is I am over-thinking and put it into a haiku. So, I made it into an activity for new poets. I have had countless new slam poets, students, and educators alike write to me after workshops and tell me that this activity is some-thing they still use themselves daily.

Modifications: Haiku for Heart Poem Activity–Growth to Flowering Plant

Primary Challenge:

Modifying this activity for little new slam poets is an exercise in knowing what they can do in terms of syllables and counting. If your little new poets are capable of syllable counting, you can absolutely do this activity as is. For those who aren't up to speed with syllable counting yet, I give them an experience word, as in a word for a specific experience they may have had. I'll sit them in a circle and say, "Think about a family holiday (or special moment) you had. Think about all the smells, sounds, tastes, and moments. Think about how all of that feels and choose one word, the biggest and best word that comes to mind. Then we're going to go in a circle and you're going to tell us what one word you think of when you think of that moment!" Sometimes I have them close their eyes as part of the experience to make sure they can really imagine their feelings and images and so they can feel less intimidated about saying their single word to the group.

Upping the Poetic Challenge:

To challenge older new slam poets, I ask them to shift their emotional perspective on the moment and write haikus about the same thing with varying intention. For example, if they choose to write about a trip to Disneyland, I challenge them to write one (or two) haiku(s) from a clearly positive emotional perspective. Then, I ask them to shift their emotional perspective and write a haiku (or two) about the same experience from a clearly negative emotional perspective. When they present them, it should be clear to the audience that they're both the same experience with a different emotional take.

GET A SENSE OF ME: A POEM FOR THE SENSES

Listen, nobody *nose* you better than you do. The way I *see* it, you should really get a *taste* for what it *feels* like to have people know you better through the senses we share. Every experience is unique to us. It is what makes us wonderfully individual! Another part of what makes us human is the desire to connect with and understand one another. Because you are someone who is absolutely worth getting to know, the challenge here is expressing how you see yourself using the senses in a way that will help people understand you. For example, LeBron James might tell people that being LeBron James smells like the rubber of brand new basketballs or fresh kicks right out of the box. Dwayne "the Rock" Johnson might tell people that being the Rock feels like the cold grip of metal gym bars or the press of heavy weights. Beyoncé might tell people that being Beyoncé sounds like the roaring stadium of thousands singing along with her or the soft breathing of her sleeping baby curled close to her ear on a night off from performing. If we close our eyes and imagine, these are all things we could get a sense of without really experiencing it.

The challenge is to use all five senses and the deep knowledge you have of yourself to help people understand what it is like to be you, then you will present yourself in a sensory poem!

STEP 1

Fill in the grid below. Try to be as specific and detailed as you can; really build up the image in the mind of your audience!

The Sense	What Being You Is Like through Those Senses
Being me smells like. . .	
Being me sounds like. . .	
Being me tastes like. . .	
Being me feels like. . . (touch, not emotion)	
Being me looks like. . .	

STEP 2

Make it a poem! Take all the images, sensations, and ideas you've jotted down and organize, arrange, and connect them to make them sentences. Make those basic building blocks into something really strong that sounds good and clearly shows off what it feels like to be you through all of your senses!

STEP 3

Get ready to present! Take a few minutes to read over, edit, and think about what the best version of your senses poem is, and get ready to show it off!

STEP 4

Poetry time! Get up, speak the truth of your senses, and teach people what it is like to be you.

STEP 5

Feel proud and awesome about your work because you absolutely should!

Modifications: Get a Sense of Me Poem Activity–Growth to Flowering Plant

Primary Challenge:

For younger new poets, I simply modify to the level of their writing. If they need a writing-free modification, I get them in a circle and talk through each sense with some examples thrown in. I ask each little poet what it sounds like to be them, and we go around the circle, sharing our ideas. I've heard everything from "Being me sounds like my cat purring because she always purrs when she cuddles me" to "Being me tastes like all the chicken nuggets because I eat so many chicken nuggets I basically AM a chicken nugget." There are many ways to catalog and present this as a collaborative community poem as well.

Upping the Poetic Challenge:

To level this activity up, you must think both inside and outside of yourself. I have the new poets get into pairs or small groups and use the handout provided as an interview sheet. They ask each other about the first sensations that come to mind. They take quick notes, then they write, armed with the basic sensory information from another new poet in the room. Then, I instruct them to do edit check-ins (at least two), where they talk with their subject, get feedback on the things they're writing, and make sure the subject feels like it's accurate. Then, they present their piece of sensory poetry to the rest of the group. I once had a student ask if they could write about their grandfather and his perspective on what it was like to experience and live through Parkinson's disease. I've included the exceptional piece below, and I encourage you to always be open to new poets using upgrades because they often offer meaningful, new perspectives.

This activity balances two great human needs: the need to be seen, heard, and valued as a human being and the need to feel safe in our skin. It fits perfectly here as a germination activity because it straddles that shifting border between individual empowerment and community building.

In the brilliant student examples that follow, notice that there is less of a focus on the spelling because the sounding out of the words was a classroom priority, and knowing that the focus was on the message gave the new poets the chance to really home in on the biggest ideas they could think of.

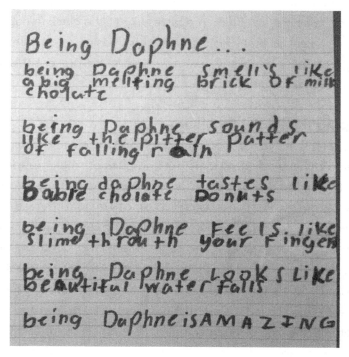

Daphne (Grade 2)

What would it be like to know the
person you never got to know?

To see them walk instead of
stiffen and their condition
worsen?

To hear them talk instead of
mumble?

To smell the warm, inviting, smell
of their home instead of a hospital?

For them to eat familiar food
instead of meals from the cafeteria.

For them to feel the soft carpet
instead of a hard, cold tile
floor?

What would it be like for their
Parkinsons to go away and to
never have to dream for them to
be their old self again?

Side note: this poem is about
my grandpa having Parkinson's
diesaes. He had it for eleven
years, until recently his
condition really worsened.
He is now in the hospital.

Emma (Grade 7)

THE FIRST POEM I EVER WROTE

You were a poet well before you knew you were. The job of a poet is to take a moment or experience and express the feelings of it. You have been letting the people around you know how you feel about things long before you knew you what you were doing!

This will be a challenge in two ways. One, you will do some research on the people around you, the people who know you, and uncover some stories about yourself before you knew who you were (from early childhood). These will prove what an exceptional poet you've always been! Two, you'll organize that into an awesome new poem, letting the people in your life know exactly why you've always been the poet you are.

STEP 1

Your challenge is to speak to the people who have known you the longest; hopefully, you'll even be able to talk to people who remember you before you remember yourself. You'll need to collect stories and moments from other people for this. You'll need to talk to them about *you*. This is a research challenge where you will be collecting stories about yourself. Think about the people who know you, love you, have stories to share about you. Ask them about those stories, then take notes on all the best pieces you hear.

Here is a list of potential questions you could ask:

- What was the first object you remember me really loving? How did you know I really loved it before I could physically tell you?
- What was the first thing you remember me being afraid of? How did you know I was afraid? How did I show you?
- Tell me a story about one of the first times you remember me being really happy. How did you know I was so happy?
- Tell me a story about the first thing I really loved or hated eating. How did you know how I felt? What did I do?

- Tell me a story about me having big feelings about something before I could tell you how I felt. How did I show you what I was feeling before I could use words to tell you?
- How did I show you how I felt before I could speak?

STEP 2

Once you have collected all of those wonderful stories and moments, it is now your job to put them together into one presentation, one poem that tells the story of you. It is important that your audience understands the experience of the things you are including. Challenge yourself to really make the experience one where they can almost put themselves in your shoes and experience what you experienced when you were writing your "first" poems.

STEP 3

Always edit, evolve, rehearse, and prepare.

STEP 4

Present! Present your "first" poem. Knock the socks off of your audience. I'll offer suggestions in the final chapter for this. Then, listen and support others the same way. That's what poets do!

Modifications: The First Poem I Ever Wrote Poem Activity–Growth to Flowering Plant

Primary Challenge:

To maintain the elements of connection and story collection, I make the task smaller. I send home a smaller instruction sheet that asks each poet to go home and collect *three* stories about themselves. I typically say, "Get a person at home to tell you a story about something you loved when you were a baby. How did they know you loved it?" Then, I ask the same question with other emotions, like things they *didn't* like or moments where they felt happy. The emotion is less important than the how. The emphasis should always be on asking *how* the person they ask knew what their younger self was feeling. That's where the idea of being a poet comes in, that ability to express experience and emotion.

Upping the Poetic Challenge:

I ask the poets who need a deeper challenge to shift their storytelling lens and tell their stories from the perspective of one of the objects that came up in their interviews. One of the best examples I've had was from a student who did the research, heard all the stories about herself, and wrote a poem from the perspective of a stuffed animal that became progressively more worn and beat up as it was carried around everywhere.

An Additional but Exceedingly Important Note:

This activity can and often is a very positive one, but it can't be ignored that some students with unique backgrounds and/or home structures may struggle with this. It is very important to be aware of your poets' backgrounds, as some may not be able to readily access people who knew them in their early childhood. New poets in foster care or who were adopted may be unable to get information like this. There are a few paths you can take here. One, you can speak with the new poet and create a list of people who may know them and are capable of sharing any stories or moments about them. This is a great opportunity, if done with care and consideration, to show a new poet that there are consistent people around them who have positive things to say about who they are. Secondly, you can change the time frame and have the new poet collect stories from people who are currently in their lives. Foster families, social workers, educational assistants, or even you as the educator can prompt them to tell stories and share moments that demonstrate who they are now and why they're currently an amazing person whose stories and poems matter.

This activity is the pinnacle of collaborative storytelling. It ends up being an artifact that new poets are proud of and connected to that shows there are people who see and value them. Here is a phenomenal student example!

Dino the stuffy with the soft purple fur. I carried you around everywhere I went.

My eyes open wide as I first experience thunder. The terror big enough to last my childhood.

Birthday parties always made me happy. You could see the excitement in my eyes during "Happy Birthday." My favorite part, however, was always the party favors.

Too afraid of the dark to go anywhere near the basement, unsure of what may be down there. Too many nightmares, unable to open the door even a crack.

I have always had a hatred for eggs and a love for mango. I've always been a particularly picky eater, though that has stayed the same my whole life.

The greatest thrill I used to have was hide-and-seek with Grandpa. I'd run around the corner. When I found him, he'd chase me back to the end of the house.

—Ava (Grade 8)

Here's another incredible student example (I can't help myself; they're so good!):

Though I was not able to say it, my parents knew they had a loving and gentle daughter. I was always really gentle with my stuffies. I always made sure they all had a spot on my bed. Even though I wasn't able to fully communicate when I was really little, my imagination was just as good. I remember the days when my parents' bed was actually a boat. Then, the sharks and crocodiles would come attack. My parents knew I was happy once they saw the smile on my young face. They also knew whenever I was feeling scared. I wasn't able to let them know with words, but with crying and holding my stuffies close. I remember putting my stuffies over my face during movies when someone was in trouble. My parents knew I liked sweets the moment I tried chocolate pudding. The empty container and chocolate all over my face did the talking for me. Things were so simple back then; I barely needed to communicate to anyone.

—Paige (Grade 8)

A LOVE POEM TO YOURSELF: A POEM IN THREE PARTS

The truth is, you are fantastic. Each and every one of you, for different, unique, and wonderful reasons, is an awesome human being. Sometimes it's hard for human beings to see their own awesomeness, so you will be given the time to write a love poem to yourself, because you deserve it. It will be a love poem in three parts: past, present, and future. You're going to write a love poem to the person you were, the person you are, and the person you hope and imagine yourself becoming later in your life.

STEP 1

All you have to do is embrace the fact that you are an amazing human person. There are so many reasons why you are amazing. Fact. Period.

STEP 2

In the grid provided below, there will be sections for the past, present, and future. Your job is to think about each of those times in your life and fill it with as many things as you like about yourself from those moments. Did you learn how to ride a bike, swim, or both when you were younger? Put it in the things you love about yourself from the past. Are you currently someone who loves to draw, play basketball, or make music? Put it in the things you love about yourself in the present. Do you picture yourself being someone amazing? Do you imagine you'll be someone who writes a great book or movie? Put it in the things you love about what you could be in the future. This is a love letter to yourself. Embrace and own what you like about yourself.

Time	Reasons/things you like about yourself (Fill it up as much as possible!)
Things you love about yourself from the past	
Things you currently love about yourself	
Things you love about who you could be	

STEP 3

Take all those fantastic things you love about your fantastic self and build them into a brilliant, poetic three-part love letter to yourself. The first stanza should be about the past, the second should be about the present, and you'll finish it all up with a stanza to yourself in the future!

STEP 4

Always edit, evolve, rehearse, and prepare.

STEP 5

Present! Present your love poem to yourself. Absolutely wow your audience. Then, listen and support others the same way. That's what slam poets do!

Modifications: A Love Poem to Yourself Poem Activity–Growth to Flowering Plant

Primary Challenge:

To modify this activity, I take away the expectation of past and future, and I encourage the new poets to focus on the now. The activity is still a love poem to the self, but I streamline it by asking questions like "What are five reasons why you're amazing?" You can document these however you'd like, but I typically instruct little new poets to write them down (or I write them down for them, depending on their writing level) and decorate their pages so they can have a really nice keepsake for when they need a reminder that there is so much to love about them.

Upping the Poetic Challenge:

Admittedly, the older poets get, the more reticent they seem to be in expressing their love for themselves and documenting it, let alone presenting it. In the interest of both upgrading the challenge and setting the precedent for self-love poetry, I encourage the new poets to study the famous piece "Invictus" by William Earnest Henley.

Invictus

Out of the night that covers me,
　　Black as the pit from pole to pole,
I thank whatever gods may be
　　For my unconquerable soul.

In the fell clutch of circumstance
　　I have not winced nor cried aloud.
Under the bludgeonings of chance
　　My head is bloody, but unbowed.

Beyond this place of wrath and tears
  Looms but the Horror of the shade,
And yet the menace of the years
  Finds and shall find me unafraid.

It matters not how strait the gate,
  How charged with punishments the scroll,
I am the master of my fate,
  I am the captain of my soul.

I have the new poets break the poem down and talk about how the author feels about himself. What evidence is there that this poet feels positively about who he sees in the mirror? It starts a discussion and normalizes self-love in writing before the new poets dive into the same idea for themselves. I've also used "How to Triumph Like a Girl" by Ada Limón, "Love After Love" by Derek Walcott, and other poems to discuss the idea of expressing self-love. I encourage you to find the poetry that suits your community best.

This activity is the one that is met with the most resistance during workshops. New poets of all ages sometimes have a hard time speaking positively about themselves. Sometimes they're concerned with whether or not they are demonstrating humility, while others are legitimately incapable of seeing all the things that make them wonderful. As educators, one of the most important things we can teach our learners is that they are valuable, incredible, and unique and that their existence absolutely matters. This is why this activity sits well in the chapter about growth and flowering; it allows new poets to grow more self-aware through a community blooming with the same understanding.

This badge is part of a whole. Each student can put their name on a petal and decorate it. It can also be glued into a journal if that is the way the class is approaching it. I have also used leaves as badges because they fit nicely on a classroom P.O.E.Tree, if that fits your theme better.

CHAPTER 4
POLLINATION

"I JUST WISH I WAS DEAD."
"THAT. IS. AWESOME!"

The reason I find myself so passionate about poetry and what it can do for people is because I've seen poetry change the trajectories of entire lives. I've seen it change the ways in which people see themselves. I've seen the power in the community it creates once it grows and blooms.

Throughout my teaching career, I've been lucky enough to lead poetry slam teams both within and outside of schools. These poetry slam teams, like any other teams, meet regularly to train and work with their teammates to prepare for competitive poetry slams. Don't forget, as much as all of this is a form unto itself, slam poetry can be a very competitive thing, where poets train hard to memorize, edit, and make sure every movement and choice counts toward their three minutes with the audience that will score them. These teams and I meet after school, sometimes at lunch or in the evening, whatever works best for practice and workshopping. It's pretty common for slam poets to bring their friends, or for other people who identify as poets to come by, read, write, and give feedback, but everyone there is serious about poetry as a craft and art form.

One of these slam team meetings took place in my classroom after school, with my team of poets and their social circles slowly streaming in. I, of course, am the prototypical "cool" teacher with my feet up on a table, my wheeled chair precariously tilted under my overconfidently angled backside. I was casually chatting with poets, listening to new ideas and edits, and being told which slam poetry videos I "have to watch," when my door was thrown open with such gusto that it hammered into the wall. Everyone froze in place and looked up to see two students: one, a member of the poetry slam team; the other, a new face. The slam team member, who we'll call Priscilla, pushed the newbie in front of her with gentle hands and introduced her like she was a trophy fish.

"Guys!" Priscilla cheered through a giant smile. "This is Gertrude, and she wishes she was dead!"

Now, Gertrude's name is not Gertrude; it has been changed for anonymity and has no bearing on this young person's desire to live, but Gertrude waved sheepishly, a half smile on her face inside of a slightly embarrassed look. She looked ahead and said, "Yeah. That's accurate." And in the impossible silence of that statement and the ensuing confusion on how to react, you could hear a pin trying not to drop. That was when my "cool" tilted chair and I fell backward onto the floor.

I did not get up. I couldn't. So I took a deep breath and said, "Gertrude, welcome. Priscilla, explain." Priscilla settled, softly closed the door behind her, and asked Gertrude if it was all right that she shared the story. Gertrude agreed. This story started in the washroom, as so many classic tales do. Priscilla had come in and taken a stall, unaware of Gertrude's presence. Priscilla, thinking she was alone, was surprised to hear what sounded like stifled crying coming from a few stalls over. Priscilla, not known for shyness, called over.

Gertrude answered, "I'm sorry. I'm just being stupid. It's nothing." Priscilla was not OK with that. She felt compelled to do more for the crying voice in the stall.

"It's obviously not nothing," Priscilla assured her. "Crying in the bathroom is very something. A few times I even—You know what? This is super weird. Do you want to just meet at the sinks and chat?"

And they did. Gertrude had explained that she felt so alone some days. She admitted that she had thought about suicide, but she knew that wasn't what this was. She didn't want to hurt herself; she just wanted a life where things felt less heavy. There was so much pressure—socially, within her family, and within herself. It was overwhelming.

She looked at Priscilla with teary eyes and said, "I mean it. I don't want to kill myself; it's just sometimes, when everything feels like too much, I wish it was over, like I had done the job and could be done with it. I just wish I was dead."

That's a big thing for a kid to have to admit to herself or anyone else. Priscilla changed from a look of concern to a look of sheer elation, took Gertrude by the hand, and said, "That. Is. Awesome!"

I started getting up and dusting myself off to put all of my support into helping Gertrude when Priscilla explained why she said what she did.

"I know that sounds bad, but I explained to her that it's awesome that she feels that big and is able to talk to me about it because I knew I had the right place for her. *Here.* It's like you've said, Mr. Johnston, great slam poets come to listen as much if not more than they come to be heard. Great slam poets know that every poem matters. You say the more we try to lift each other up, the stronger all of our backs get, so I knew Gertrude could be a great slam poet, and I knew we could all be better for it. This is, like, the big feels club."

The Big Feels Club. It was a moment where I saw the power of a community with an open-door policy built on honest caring and support. When you make your intentions clear, have positive access points, and the tools to set it up step by step (remember, that's how the New Kids on the Block suggested you show people you really want them in your world), you can build a community for new slam poets around new slam poets. Slam poetry can be an essential community for new slam poets even when they don't know they are slam poets just yet. It can be a sports team for people who don't play sports. Though it is open to everyone, sometimes you'll get a Troy Bolton or two. Both kinds of teams need people who embrace being in this together, a lesson best, and most musically, expressed in *High School Musical*. Poetry can be a place for the kids who scribble on crumpled paper scraps when they're feeling too much to focus in classes and need a socially positive outlet. It is for any and everyone because it requires nothing more than the poem you are writing and the need to connect.

This chapter is themed around the plant phase of pollination for that reason. A community can't really thrive and become the best version of itself unless it is open to interacting with the world around it. We've taken the time to plant seeds, germinate, grow, and bloom into a garden; now comes the time when our community interacts with the larger world and becomes a part of something even bigger and more significant. In fact, many plants can't bear fruit or achieve the highest limits of their potential without interacting with pollinators. This chapter will focus on how a community of new poets can become both self-sufficient in its motivation and continue to grow in its meaning and scope of impact through metaphorical pollination. Some plants and new poets will be self-pollinating, but many count on outside pollinators to move through their transformative stages. Without outside pollinators, there are legions of tasty fruits and vegetables and beautiful flowers that wouldn't exist.

POET ACTIVITY: POLLINATION (EDUCATOR SUPPORT)

STEP 1

Reflect. Take time to celebrate what you've done and identify what your next steps might look like. It's OK to look over earlier parts of this guide and do more of the activities intended for other chapters, especially since these chapters are designed to give opportunities for growth and progress, which is what you and your community of new poets are striving toward. It is always OK to build on that. Every next step should feel like a conscious decision to move forward.

Remember, nobody is ever going to read this unless you show them. There is no better way to learn than to have something not work and evolve through it. What didn't work? What would you have done differently? What are you going to fail forward from?

_____

_____

_____

Now, flip that coin. (Don't worry about humility. Remember, nobody is going to see this.) And remember that it's important to see where the strong points are so you can build on them. What did you do right? How did you absolutely rock that last chapter? Why are you an awesome new poet and how did you help new poets germinate?

_____

_____

_____

STEP 2

Make a plan for the next steps!

In the last chapter, as they were living between their individual growth and the vulnerability and faith involved in becoming a member of a community, your students needed you to be flexible and see their needs, see them as people, and adapt. Here, as the metaphor of pollination has them opening up what you have built together in a variety of ways, you will likely look more like a solid waypoint, a place of safety as the community grows and interacts with the larger ecosystem.

This chapter's role is one of facilitation, one of making pollination a possibility for the plants in your room who need more than the tight-knit community you've built to help them reach their full potential and become what they're meant to become. Your little community of poets will be more than enough for a percentage of your new poets, but some voices need more. As we build, we need to ask, "Is what we are doing P.O.E.Tree?" You've put in the work to seed, germinate, and grow the incredible new poet voices around you. As they gain momentum and purpose, let's make sure our intentions match that evolution. Let's make sure all of this is truly P.O.E.Tree.

P—**Pericardial:** While the last chapter had you taking on the role of a caring and patient gardener, in this chapter, your garden needs things beyond itself. Demonstrating how close new poet voices are to your heart is more an act of showing them how much faith you have that others will see and hear that same value. The best possible way to show your new poets just how close to your heart they are is by finding ways to have others see their value. This is the step that takes them from feeling good because they know who they are is close to your heart to feeling like they can change the world because of the potential for the power of their voices to connect them to someone else's pericardium.

How are you going to make sure that your love for their voices and truths is infectious? How are you going to provide opportunities for others to hold what these new poets have to say close to their hearts? How are you going to make sure your community, space, and you yourself still feel safe and close, while also providing opportunities for the incredible people blooming in your little garden to put themselves out there?

I will. . .

_____

_____

_____

◯ **—Open:** In the last chapter, being open looked like meaningfully supporting the truth of students' voices. Remember, being open is about being honestly willing to hear how these individuals want to be seen, embracing how they view themselves, and checking your assumptions or preconceptions. It is their responsibility to put their truth out there, and it becomes your responsibility to help others be as open to their truth as you've been. As an added challenge, you also have to build a sense of openness for your community. With you as the gardener, your community has to be willing to allow pollinators to fly in and out. A voice is meant to be shared. It is important to be open to ways in which others can come into the community, both as invited guests and as those in need of their voices being heard.

How will you make sure you are open to your new poets growing beyond what you've built? How will you make your community truly open and propagate the idea that people who need their voices to be heard can come and interact with you and your new poets to start their own journey toward that validation?

I will. . .

_____

_____

_____

E **—Electrifying:** It takes electricity and emotional work to develop new poets from seed to full-on fire-spitting poet. As the poets gain strength and value in their voices, I find it's important to be really open to the two-way flow of electricity. Of course, you have to always pour your own electricity into making the poetry engine run, but the beauty of empowered new poets feeling like their voices need to be out there means their energy will also help power it all. Be open to electricity that equals your own. Seek it out. Empower the electricity of the blooming agents of this community and use every watt from your collective passion to charge forward.

How are you going to make sure that electricity is a two-way street that welcomes and embraces the passion coming from all directions? How will you harness it? How will you make sure all that electricity is both contagious and specifically focused and useful?

I will. . .

T—Tree: This is the soul of this chapter. In the last chapter, you were challenged to think about how to grow both the individual and the community simultaneously. Here, the question is how will you help your poets grow beyond the community you've helped create? Wherever you've done this work (classroom and community), the task is now to make sure the work you've done always has a healthy sense of growth.

How are you going to make sure that what you've helped build has the opportunity and inspiration to grow beyond itself? How are you going to make sure your new poets have the ownership and agency to get their voices out into the larger ecosystem? How will you make sure your new poet community is open and welcoming to both new voices and new audiences?

I will. . .

Things I want to remember when mapping this out (Notes to Self):

_____

_____

_____

Remember, you don't have to have all the answers right away; this is just a prompt to help you think honestly about where you are in this moment.

STEP 3

Consider the implications of both collaborative storytelling and emotional mindfulness. I want to talk about a world champion slam poet, friend, and all-around incredible human being, Ian Keteku. If you have no knowledge of Ian Keteku, find some of his work online and listen to one of the greatest slam poets of all time, and as he would say, "give thanks."

Collaborative Storytelling

Ian Keteku is a great collaborative storyteller, and I bring him up specifically in this chapter because he is the one who showed me that there is a point where your story, the stories you've helped inspire, and the community wrapped around both all need to find their space in the world outside of themselves. Mr. Keteku is a world champion slam poet. He pours so much of what that title and subsequent career have been into building up the community around him. He has coached teams that also became national champions, he has dedicated himself to youth poets and their burgeoning voices, and his story has allowed him to help others write their own stories.

Mr. Keteku showed me that collaborative storytelling is about those who get to write chapters and the process of passing the pen. By welcoming in pollinators and other connections to the larger ecosystem, new poets and growing, blooming poets found ways in which their voices could become the next chapter through the earlier chapters written by their mentor. I have seen Mr. Keteku take over entire concert halls with the power of his slam poetry artistry, but it was something else to see him standing in the shadows in the back of the room at poetry slams where youth poets he mentored and coached were absolutely crushing it. He is a world champion who has stood back with a look in his eye that showed a collaborative storyteller who understands there is power in his voice, words, and experiences but something infinitely deeper in weaving his story alongside those of others, impacting who they are as poets moving forward. That's legacy. That's who you have the potential to be.

Your P.O.E. Tree directly influences the poetry of those you're lucky enough to work with, and that links you in trust and care, that links you in meaning and moments. It makes you a true collaborative storyteller. Pollination is the point in collaborative storytelling when you make yourself willing to be an earlier chapter and really focus on helping blooming new poets find ways to become mentors, performers, seekers of spaces, seekers of other voices and stories, evolved versions of themselves, and so many other roles where they can slowly take the pen from your hand, and you can become more of a grateful, proud supporter and witness.

Emotional Mindfulness

Emotional mindfulness in the context of pollination is something that I find so fascinating. In the last chapter, we focused on cultivating a balance between personal vulnerability and faith in a developing community. This chapter is about being emotionally mindful enough to understand students' needs and accept whatever that looks like. If you are emotionally mindful enough, you'll be able to see which new poets are community kids and support and endorse them living comfortably in that little poetry family unit. Other voices will need other places to be heard, other classrooms, assemblies, and presentations. They'll need to know that not only are their voices heard and valued, but they can actually *do* something with those voices. These are the plants that will need outside interaction, pollination, and connection to the greater ecosystem.

A gardener can't be a honeybee. A gardener can't force roots to grow in ways that are against their nature. But a gardener can make sure they know just how important it is that the plants in their garden interact with the greater ecosystem for individual pollination and complete growth. No matter what form they come in, you need to be emotionally mindful of what that ecosystem can do for your blooming new poets.

STEP 4

Buffet time!

If you want to, go back over other sections, return to the buffets of other chapters, mix, match, mingle, or mangle, do whatever you need to do with what I am offering you to make it organic to both you and your new poets.

Make your plan, go through all that I've offered and all that I'm about to offer in this delicious buffet section, and dirty the plates the way you feel is right for you. Make the pieces of what I've given you into the right kind of monster for your new poets and the community you've built together, with a focus on access points for pollinators. How much time are you dedicating to this? Is it too much or not enough? Is there a need for a new group to form on its own, like a slam poetry club or team for the new poets who are really blooming through this? How are you making sure you're still celebrating individuals while also embracing the potential of your burgeoning community? Continue to grow and flower, but look for the pollinators and make sure to provide welcoming access points for your new poets to have their voices heard by the larger ecosystem. You have a plan and you have activities, ideas, suggestions, and supports laced through this chapter and all of the previous chapters, so dive in and dive deep!

Welcome back to the buffet! Time for another helping!

Like I've said in other buffets, you should Frankenstein this smorgasbord, pick, choose, edit, and evolve these pieces I'm offering until they're perfectly, authentically yours. Know your intentions, know your new poets, and know there is enough in here to build something really meaningful.

BUFFET

BUFFET BREAKDOWN
(ANOTHER OFFERING OF DELICIOUS ACTIVITIES)

1. **Poem in Your Pocket**—Originating through National Poem in Your Pocket Day, this is an activity that can go in several directions depending on intentions, but it is based on the concept of writing with specific, positive intention and human connection.

2. **What's Your Story?**—This activity makes poets both agents of their poetry community and masters of their potential voices.

3. **Build Your Own Echo**—This activity gets new poets thinking about how they want people to remember them when they're not around and the kind of impression and impact their words, actions, and interactions have on how they are perceived.

4. **Musically Poetic**—By using several pieces of classical music, new poets will get a chance to think about how different aspects of tone and intention get different reactions from the audience, and how they can wrap their own writing around that intention.

5. **Destroy All Poems!**—This activity takes a different look at both emotional intention and performance through that intention. New poets will look at poems written by others, evaluate the emotional intention, and experiment.

6. **Fictional Character Poetry Slam**—This is an actual poetry slam with some changed aspects for new slam poets to both create and experience a scored poetry slam, without having to put their own story out there.

7. **This Is Slam Poetry**—This activity will allow new poets to create an opinion on what "good" slam poetry is, which will allow them to build that perspective into their own writing, as well as work on their justification skills.

POEM IN YOUR POCKET

You—yes, *you*—are so powerful! You are a master of the feels, and you are capable of using your poetry to convey and share so many emotions. Your task is to write the ultimate feel-good poem. Your poem will be directly responsible for making someone feel valued, awesome, and good about who they are. Here are the steps!

STEP 1: POCKET SYSTEM, ACTIVATE!

For this activity, everyone participating in the community will need a pocket. There are tons of fun ways to do this. You can cut the pockets from old pairs of pants or make pockets out of felt, fabric, or paper. Use what you have, but make it look great; make it look like *your* pocket that's ready for some poetry!

STEP 2: WRITE AN INSPIRING, POSITIVE POEM!

Everyone deserves to hear something inspiring and positive to remind them how great they are and how great life can be. Decide as a community on the rules of your inspirational and positive poems. Are they haikus? Are they open format? Are there any rules on length? Make sure you know the rules and expectations before you start writing!

Once you have your structure, write a poem that is as inspiring as you can possibly make it. Your intention here is to pump up your reader, no matter who it is, and help them feel positive about themselves and their life. Try to think about what you might need to hear to get you inspired and fired up, to help you be the best you! (Note: don't put your name on this poem. It's top secret and anonymous!)

STEP 3: RANDOM POCKET GENERATOR

Once you've finished writing, hand your poem(s) to the leader of the activity. After they've read them over to make sure they're classroom appropriate and positive, they'll top secretly and randomly put the poems in the pockets!

STEP 4: POCKET POEM POWER!

Read the awesome poem in your pocket. Think about how this poem could get everyone pumped up. Then, being the amazing poet you are, when it's your turn, you are going to read the poem you've received like a passionately positive poet would! That will make sure everyone can soak up all that power and energy!

STEP 5: BE EVEN MORE AWESOME!

Return the favor. That's right, we're going to do it again so we can learn to feel the momentum of powerfully positive energy! The challenge? Take everything you've heard and try to be even more electrifying. How can you make your next piece the best positive and inspiring poem of all time?

Modifications: Poem in Your Pocket Activity—Pollination

Primary Challenge:

I like to call this modification "Massive Mini Poems" because poetry is about saying big things in condensed forms. If you'd like, you can complete the activity as listed in the previous hand-out, simply adjusting to cater to your class's writing level. But it's important to note that I have had great success taking this out of the classroom as well. Educators love their hallway bulletin boards. The little new poets can put up their pockets and fill them with massive mini poems. These poems are positive, kind, and inspiring, and anyone who walks by them in the hallway will see a big sign that says, "Please Take a Poem from a Pocket!" So many kids walking by will take them and be inspired.

Upping the Poetic Challenge:

I ask the new slam poets I'm working with to come together and hatch new ideas for what can inspire them. There are a few paths the modifications can take here. First, we study the work of other poets, challenging the new poets to find "famous" poets who are known for finding the beauty in the people and things around them. Challenge your new slam poets to do the same: take things that are already in the world around them and make them into absolute images of beauty and positivity.

Next, I ask them to go through the activity and build a pocket wall somewhere in the school community. I can usually find a bulletin board in need of some sprucing up and a good social positivity project. Once that wall is built and the adorable pockets adorn it, I not only have the new slam poets make posters to make it clear that any and all are welcome to take the poems, but I also challenge the kids who are embracing poetry to consistently write positive poems to fill the pockets. I challenge another classroom to be the stewards of the wall for a time, filling it with their own poems. I empower a few of my new poets to explain the project to those classes and be poetry leaders in and for their budding community.

I should note that I don't take credit for Poetry in Your Pocket at all. This concept is well above my pay grade and was originally started as an activity for National Poetry Month (which is in April) to inspire people to access and interact with poetry more meaningfully. Please exploit the many materials available for National Poetry Month.

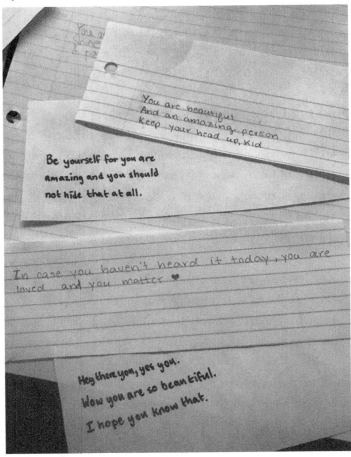

This is a gorgeous example that my middle school poets built!

WHAT'S YOUR STORY?

There is perhaps no more powerful question to ask someone than "What's your story?" Today, you are going to let someone know just how much they matter and how important it is that they exist, because they are the only one who can ever tell their story. Then, you're going to make it even better by turning their story into a poem written by a phenomenal poet (that's you!).

STEP 1: STORY SEEKING

Think of yourself as a honeybee collecting the nectar you will bring back to the hive and turn into honey. Find someone outside of the group you are working with and politely ask them, "What's your story?"

How you collect this story will take on a variety of shapes based on their comfort level and yours. Talk with the subject who is offering their story. You could film them, give them a pen and paper if they prefer to write it down, or you can take notes while they speak. It is very important to decide how both you and the storyteller can feel positive and confident about the story collection.

Once you decide together, collect that story as accurately and thoroughly as possible. Please make sure you tell them that it can be any story they want to share about their lives, as long as it is appropriate and honest! (Speaking your truth means a lot to slam poets!)

STEP 2: POEM-IFICATION

You'll take some time to build what you've heard into the best poem you can. Your intention here is to show the storyteller just how much hearing their story meant to you and how much it matters that they have stories to tell. Your job is to show them how you felt about their story. See, human stories are poetry, and each and every person should be valued for it. Writing this poem will show them just how important their existence is to the world.

STEP 3: MAKIN' IT SIZZLE

Take the time to edit and evolve. Talk to other people about your work and get feedback and ideas. Read it out loud to yourself to see how it feels and what it sounds like as an experience. Ask yourself if your piece is doing the emotional job you intended it to do. Make sure it represents you and your storyteller well!

STEP 4: PREPARE AND PRESENT

Decide as a team what the presentation will look like. It might look like individual moments, if that is more comfortable, but it could also be a fantastic small event where you and the other slam poets in the community invite the storytellers to present and celebrate the slam poetry and the stories that inspired it!

Show the storyteller just how much hearing their story meant to you and how much it matters that they have stories to tell.

Modifications: What's Your Story?
Poem Activity—Pollination

Primary Challenge:

I instruct the little new poets to choose someone they love and tell the story of why they love them. If they are too little for large-scale writing, I take notes for them like an interview. Because this activity is about sharing stories, I ask them first to tell me about someone they love, then I ask them to tell me a story about that person. I record it word for word as much as I possibly can. I then print the stories out and get the little new poets to decorate them with a picture of that person. It makes for a great gift.

Upping the Poetic Challenge:

This activity is already high level. It asks new slam poets to physically put themselves out there, become responsible for the collection and validation of someone else's story, then create a poem around their experience of that story, which they'll later present. To take the work even further, I like to wrap this one into the language of experience. We take the time to look through a few of the stories from the What's Your Story activity and talk about what makes them emotionally impactful, and I also work through a poem called "The Time Around Scars" by Michael Ondaatje.

This piece is about the meaning stories place around things, how a scar can sometimes just be a scar, but when a story is wrapped around it, every little imperfection can be a story. I like to speak to them about one of my favorite concepts, the Japanese philosophy of wabi-sabi. In essence, wabi-sabi is the idea that the imperfection and transience of a thing inherently gives it more value. Say you're having coffee with a dear friend and she chips the edge of one of your coffee cups. You wash it and put it away, but any time you open up the cabinet and see all the identical cups, the one with the chip in the side becomes your preferred cup because it makes you think of that moment you sat for coffee with your friend. That is wabi-sabi, the perfectly imperfect.

That is what these poets are seeking when they are experiencing these stories from others. They are viewing people around them as having deeper value because of the scars, chipped edges, and stories that have built into their bodies over a lifetime. The more connection and human understanding that can be exchanged through this, the more both slam poets and their community can grow. Pollination to fruition.

I want to talk to you about a book that inspired this activity. That book is called *What's Your Story? True Experiences from Complete Strangers*. It is written (kind of) by Brandon Doman. The author set up in a coffee shop and simply asked people, because he was curious, to tell him a story. He gave them paper and pen so he could have it in their words, and the only criteria he gave them was that it had to be completely honest and truthful. Every detail. What he got was magic.

That entire book is proof of what I've been preaching in this one: everyone has a poem that is being written inside them. There is nothing more meaningful and powerful to another human person than to know that someone cares to hear them speak their poem in its honesty, in their own words. This activity does just that, empowering both the poet and the subject.

BUILD YOUR OWN ECHO

What would you do if you knew exactly when you would lose your voice? The Tragically Hip is one of Canada's most famous and celebrated bands. Their front man, Gordon (Gord) Downie, was an incredible songwriter and poet. Many named him Canada's Poet because the lyrics of his songs highlighted what it was like to live as a Canadian in the most beautiful ways. When Downie was diagnosed with a terminal brain tumor in December 2015, the entire nation felt like they were going to lose one of their own. It felt like a national diagnosis.

Knowing he had limited time, Gordon Downie did something amazing. He and his band released their thirteenth and final album, *Man Machine Poem,* and they scheduled what they knew would be their final tour. That tour culminated in his final performance, which was televised and watched live by almost twelve million people.

Downie used his farewell tour as a chance to tell people how he felt about them, to tell them *why* he loved them and what things about them mattered most to him. He took the time to tell people what causes mattered most to him and what he hoped his legacy would grow into after he was gone. He had a chance to decide exactly how he would be remembered and exactly what his legacy would be. He made his poetry and his voice matter so much in the days before he was gone.

WHAT WOULD YOU DO IF YOU KNEW YOUR VOICE HAD LIMITED TIME?

This will be your challenge as a poet. We are lucky to not have to focus on the same motivations as Gord Downie. But if you knew that tomorrow you would lose your voice forever, what would you want to say to people before you couldn't say anything anymore? If you knew you wouldn't be able to speak, write, or communicate anymore, what do you feel you would need to do with your voice before it was silenced? Who would you need to communicate with? Why? What would you need people to know about you?

STEP 1: SPILL DRAFT

A spill draft is when a poet like you takes a piece of paper and, working from a writing prompt, spills onto the page as much as they possibly can in a certain amount of time. Here, the writing prompt is: What would you say if you knew this would be the last day you could speak/write/communicate? What would you need people to hear?

You won't necessarily be using all of what you write down, so just let yourself write everything down that comes to mind. This part will not be presented at all; it is a safe space to spill from your heart.

STEP 2: POEM FIRST DRAFT

Take a look at your spill draft. What stands out to you? What pieces do you want to continue to pursue and develop? What pieces feel the most important and necessary to say? Remember, this is about what you would make sure to say if you knew you would never be able to say anything else. Make sure you are approaching this activity with that lens. How do you want people to remember your voice? What do you want to know? What kind of echo will you build?

STEP 3: MAKIN' IT SIZZLE

Take the time to edit and evolve. Talk to other people about your work and get feedback and ideas. Read it out loud to yourself to see how it feels and what it sounds like as an experience. Ask yourself if your piece is doing the emotional job you intended it to do. Ask yourself, "If this was the last thing I was ever going to say, would I be satisfied by what I was saying?"

STEP 4: PREPARE AND PRESENT

You're writing with the intention of presentation. Especially with the nature of this project, be ready to speak your truth and use your voice like never before, while imagining what it might be like if this was the last thing you could say. So how do you want your voice to be remembered? What's your echo?

Modifications: Build Your Own Echo Poem Activity—Pollination

Primary Challenge:

I like to write a song with younger new poets. Now, I'm admittedly not a musician. I choose a special moment that the little new poets are sharing together (like the end of year) and choose a song we can pirate the lyrics to. Then, I work with the little new poets and have each of them build one line of lyrics into the song based on how they feel in that moment. There is potential here for them to perform it, as well, like a poetic winter concert, if that is what fits your team.

Upping the Poetic Challenge:

To upgrade, we study the lyrics and poetry of Gordon Downie and the Tragically Hip, showing the link between music and poetry. After, I like to give students a chance to review the music they like and do a study on the lyrics of their song of choice. Poets take ownership of their choices and opinions. They get to talk about *why* they chose the piece, what the intention of the writer was, and what the experience ended up being for the slam poet that chose it. Presentation is an important part of pollination, because it continues to build the validation of the individual's voice and also shows poets that poetry needs a relationship and interaction with those experiencing it.

How do you want your voice remembered?

I feel lucky to have had the inspiration for this activity brought about by an exceptional musician and poet. I credit *Maclean's* magazine with the seed of this activity. When Gordon Downie was on his final inspiring tour, telling people the why of his love, the magazine ran a promotion where Canadians could write essays specifically to their loved ones in the spirit of Downie's purpose. They called their essay series "Before I Go," and while it was specific to a person in the spirit of not leaving things unsaid, it inspired this activity in which I have new poets think about the message of their legacy.

This activity is about really considering how people hear and respond to poets and their work. When you're mindful of how the audience will perceive you and why, it adds to the methodology behind each new poet's writing process. You're almost collaboratively storytelling with your intended audience. This is emotional pollination.

MUSIC IS POETRY

Voltaire once said, "Poetry is the music of the soul." Longfellow once said, "Music is the universal language of mankind." Miley Cyrus once said, "Everyone needs a song."

No matter who said it, the truth is both poetry and music do the same job: they try to connect one person to another with a feeling and an experience. Edgar Allan Poe wants you to feel, understand, and connect with his feelings of guilt and fear. Taylor Swift wants you to feel, understand, and connect with her feelings after a breakup. It's all about human connection through emotional experience; it's just done through different art forms.

Your poet challenge today will be to link those two art forms.

STEP 1

The poet leading the activity will play several classical music pieces for you. They will not tell you anything about these pieces ahead of time. Your job will be to listen and let yourself feel and imagine. In the spaces provided below, spill out as many words or thoughts as you can while the music is playing. What does it make you feel? What does it make you picture or imagine? The next steps of the activity will be easier the more you write, so dive in and fill the boxes with as many words, thoughts, feelings, and images as you can that are inspired by the music you are listening to. When you've done each piece, you'll shift gears and do it all over again for a completely different piece of music!

Name of Music Piece	Your Thoughts, Feelings, Images, and Ideas

STEP 2

Choose your favorite piece of music and corresponding responses. Pick the one that spoke to you, the one where you really felt the music and your words and images come together to form something fantastic.

STEP 3

Time to write, poet! Put your best work into developing a great first draft of a poem. Think about what overall impression you want to give. Connect with your audience! Since this is a first draft, be ready for feedback and improvement!

STEP 4

After a set period of writing time, you'll meet with the new poets who chose the same piece of music you did as your inspiration. How you meet, the group size, and the length of time will all be decided by the leader of this activity.

Be a listener. Really give each poet the time and space to speak. Respect their voice as much as they will respect yours. Provide feedback with honesty and kindness. Remember, too, that you should balance the things you like about a piece with the suggestions you have. Put yourself out there and give it your best!

STEP 5

Once you've had a chance to work with your feedback group, work on edits and make your poem into the best possible poem you can!

STEP 6

Spit fire! Present! The music will be played for you, and you will present your poem on top of it like it was the soundtrack to your epic poem!

STEP 7

Enjoy your success and support other new poets as they get up and present!

Modifications: Music Is Poetry
Poem Activity—Pollination

Primary Challenge:

To modify this activity, I forgo the need for the poets to write down their experiences. Instead, I play a piece of music and ask them to move (safely) around the room in the way the music inspires them to. There is no wrong way to do this. Once the songs are over, they sit and I ask them to share all the words, thoughts, ideas, and images each piece of music gave them. I then write all those words on a large piece of paper or on the whiteboard, and that becomes our collective poem about how those pieces made us feel and what we imagined together. When I have time, I also let them decorate the paper with colors and images, then I hang it on the wall to display the poem we wrote together.

Upping the Poetic Challenge:

To create a challenge, I change the steps of the activity. I assign new poets to random groups, and each group gets a randomly chosen piece of music. As much as possible, each song is kept secret from the other groups. Then, as a team, each group gets the time and space to listen to those pieces and follow the same process as the activity handout, with the end goal of collaborating for the final piece. I like to call it a "symphonic sound study," and I explain that all voices are like instruments that need to come together harmoniously.

I also have a personal soundtrack warm-up activity that I love, where I ask the new poets several questions, like:

- You are a flower. What song is playing while you bloom and why?
- You are a cold, hard block of ice. What song is playing while you melt and why?
- You are feeling your biggest possible feels. What song is playing while you react and why?

> Responding to questions like these really gets students thinking about their emotional intention, as well as how they respond to and contextualize emotional information through music.

Linking the intention of poetry with the intention of music helps new slam poets understand the value of using the emotional tools at their disposal to connect with other people. Beautiful music is out there en masse, but it's important for this activity to avoid pieces with lyrics, as that tends to overtell the story and influence what the new poets come up with.

Some amazing music suggestions include:
- "Claire de Lune"—Debussy
- "Summer"—Vivaldi
- "Waltz of the Flowers"—Tchaikovsky
- Gymnopédie No. 1—Satie
- *Peter and the Wolf*—Prokofiev
- *Rhapsody in Blue*—Gershwin

I also love using iconic musical scores from films like:
- *The Good, the Bad and the Ugly*—Ennio Morricone
- *Inception* (especially "Time")—Hans Zimmer
- *The Last of the Mohicans*—Trevor Jones
- *Schindler's List*—John Williams
- *Robin Hood: Prince of Thieves*—Michael Kamen
- *Forrest Gump*—Alan Silvestri
- *The Chronicles of Narnia: The Lion, the Witch and the Wardrobe* (especially "The Battle Song")— Harry Gregson-Williams
- *Meet Joe Black* (especially "Whisper of a Thrill")— Thomas Newman

This activity can easily be spaced over several classes. Please make sure you give enough time for a deep dive into the music they're experiencing. This might look like dedicating the first class to the first steps and another class to working through it.

DESTROY ALL POEMS!

All forms of poetry have emotional intention, which is a fancy way of saying that each and every poem has a feeling it is trying to get across. That's how you know a love poem is a love poem and an epic poem is an epic poem. To gain a better understanding of this concept, today we're going to figure out what a poem's emotional intention is, and we're going to flip it upside down!

STEP 1: EXAMPLES (FOR PRACTICE)

How do you read an angry poem so people *know* it is an angry poem? How can you make sure the intended emotions come through when you read?

Now . . . it's time for destruction!

STEP 2: DESTROY THE EMOTIONAL INTENTION!

Now that you understand how to read a poem the way it was meant to be read, it is time to think about how you could totally change the emotional intention of that piece by deciding on a completely different emotion and making that your focus. For extra fun, you may want to write a bunch of emotions or emotional intentions (happy, sad, silly, dramatic) onto pieces of paper and randomly draw them to challenge yourself.

Choose a piece of poetry (or have one assigned to you by the poet in charge of the activity), figure out the original emotional intention, then *destroy* that intention by preparing to present it in a completely different way. For example, read the "I Am Angry" poem in a happy manner!

STEP 3: PRESENT!

When your time comes, you'll start by presenting your poem with its original emotional intention. That way, your audience will know not only the work, but also the original emotion and that you're great at breaking down and understanding poetry. Then, hit the audience with a completely different emotional take!

Modifications: Destroy All Poems!
Poem Activity–Pollination

Primary Challenge:

I only slightly modify from the activity above. We are lucky we have myriad books these days that help students understand their emotional needs, so I start with those books and really dive deep into what we know about the emotions in those books. If the little new poets are old enough, I have them write short poems with specific emotional intentions and have the other little new poets in class guess how they feel and explain why. If they are not ready to write short pieces themselves, then I help them out.

A list of really great books that focus on acknowledging and managing feelings include:

- *The Feelings Book*–Todd Parr
- *The Sad Little Fact*–Jonah Winter
- *When Sadness Is at Your Door*–Eva Eland
- *Grumpy Monkey*–Suzanne and Max Lang
- *My Heart*–Corinna Luyken
- *Glad Monster, Sad Monster*–Ed Emberley
- *Happy Hippo, Angry Duck*–Sandra Boynton

Upping the Poetic Challenge:

I follow the same criteria as the activity handout, but I challenge them to rewrite the entire poem they're working with to show off that new emotional intention, while maintaining the integrity of the story itself. For example, if they're rewriting a love poem from a few hundred years ago into an epic masterpiece or a tale of frustration and anger, it still has to tell the story the original piece did, and it can't involve ninjas or aliens. It is important ask check-in questions to gear their writing brains, like:

- What is the story here?
- How are you making sure you're keeping the story the same?
- Why do you think the people in and around this poem feel the way they do? How do you know?
- What words in the poem need to stay the same? Which ones need to be replaced? Why do you feel this way?
- What is the new emotion you've chosen here? How are you going to make sure the story remains intact while portraying a new emotional experience?
- Why did you choose the new emotion you did? What do you hope your audience will experience through this new telling of the same story?

This activity was inspired by a scientific education expedition. I was lucky enough to be named as a National Geographic Grosvenor Teacher Fellow, partially because of my slam poetry work, and because of it, I got the chance to travel far and wide. One particular journey was to the Galápagos Islands, where I ran a poetry workshop on the equator, leading everyone on the vessel to write poetry about how it felt to be in one of the last places where nature can grow freely. I asked them to use their senses to connect their experience to others. Many of the people I worked with on the vessel wrote about the taste of salt on their lips and how much they liked it. Then, one writer stood to share and talked about how the salt spray of the ocean was something he couldn't stand because it tasted like overprocessed, oversalted food. It made him feel like the sea life we'd been working with could be processed and eaten, just like anywhere else in the world. People were floored. What a unique perspective! There are so many things that connect us and seem universal, but those very things have the potential to be unique and specific to a person and their experience. This activity is wrapped around how that salt can taste different to each poet.

FICTIONAL CHARACTER POETRY SLAM!

It's time for an awesome, real deal, fully competitive poetry slam—your storytelling versus everyone else's, your presentation style versus everyone else's, your onstage action and ability to connect to an audience against everyone else's!

We're going to run a legitimate poetry slam together, but with some major twists!

1. Only *one* of your slam poems will be scored, with the highest scorer declared the champion for this particular slam!

2. While typical poetry slams have five judges issuing scores, this poetry slam will have a roomful of judges. Everyone is a judge in this slam!

3. While you typically get three minutes to perform in poetry slams, you will get only two minutes in this one! Make every word count!

4. While a typical poetry slam has a rule against using costumes and props, in this poetry slam, feel free to bring in whatever costumes and props you want!

5. Finally, and here is the biggest and most fun twist: typically in a poetry slam, you bring material you've written from your own story, but this slam will be a fictional character slam, meaning you'll either choose or be assigned a fictional character from a book, movie, show, game, or comic! You'll have the opportunity to write from the perspective of that character, and you will be them during this poetry slam!

STEP 1

You will either choose or be assigned a fictional character (depending on what the poet leading the activity decides), but either way, there can be no doubles! For example, there cannot be two Harry Potters in the poetry slam, nor can there be two Spider-Mans.

STEP 2

Once you have your fictional character, you'll have the time to write an awesome slam poem from their perspective. Put yourself in their shoes. Remember, this isn't your slam poem; it's *their* slam poem. What would Mickey Mouse say in his slam poem? What would Darth Vader say in his slam poem? You are your character in their slam poem. You wouldn't write that Kermit the Frog loved playing the banjo; you would say, "I love the feeling of banjo strings humming in my green froggy fingers."

STEP 3

Edit, improve, and prepare to present.

STEP 4

Slam time! The person in charge of the activity will decide the order of the slam. It might be random, alphabetical, or by assigned character. Be ready!

Once it's your turn, slam your best possible slam poem performance in the persona of your fictional character.

Judges After each amazing slam poem, you as an audience member will become a judge! The poet leading the activity will ask everyone (on the count of three, so other people's votes don't influence their own) to raise *one* hand, and on that one hand, you will give a score of one through five with your fingers. The poet leading the activity will then add up the score from the room for each fictional character slam poem!

STEP 5

Declare a champion! Once the scores are added up in the room, the fictional character with the highest score will become the poetry slam champion! If there is a tie, the poet in charge will decide how the tie will be broken. (For educators: I suggest going with a sudden-death haiku, where the poets write a haiku from the perspective of their fictional characters and the audience votes for the best one, but there are a lot of great ways to break a tie!)

STEP 6

Celebrate! You and your fellow slam poets did amazing work here. How will you celebrate each other?

Modifications: Fictional Character Poetry Slam Activity–Pollination

Primary Challenge:

Rather than having little new poets write independently, I like to discuss what fictional characters are as a starting point. We chat about a few characters they know, and I project large pictures and ask them questions that put them inside the perspectives of these characters, like "What do you think Spider-Man thinks about?" "How do you think Super Mario feels?" or "What do you think makes Pikachu happy?" I take note of their responses and turn them into "I am . . ." statements. Then, I help the little new poets read those poems aloud.

Upping the Poetic Challenge:

To upgrade, I invite students to dress up, bring props, and dive completely into the characters they are working with. It makes for awesome, dramatic, and play-based learning. I have also upgraded this to be a study of specific book characters or historical figures they are studying. For example, when celebrating military holidays, such as Remembrance Day in Canada or Veterans Day in the United States, I have often given the new poets the names of actual soldiers, or I have asked them to think of members of their families that have served. From there, I ask them to put themselves into the perspectives of those soldiers and incorporate the information they find into their piece. I also ask them to make the presentation meaningful and beautiful; that's always an upgrade.

"When they took me away from my family at age 14, they said it will be "ok".
When they suited me up with green clothes and handed me a weapon, they said it will be "ok".
When they shoved me on a plane and told me to be quiet, they said it will be "ok".
When they dumped me in some country and left, there was no one to tell me it was going to be "ok".
When they flew over top of me and released a gas, I told myself it was going to be "ok".
When the gas caught up to me and stabbed me in the chest, I told myself I was going to be "ok".
When they took me away from my family at age 14, they said that I would see them again.
It wasn't ok."

—John

Bella (Grade 7)

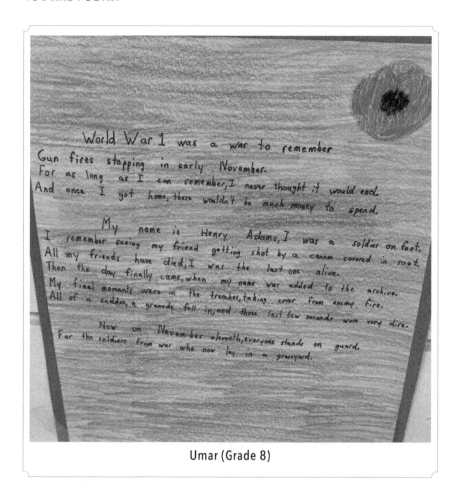

Umar (Grade 8)

This activity has all the elements of a true poetry slam, but it has the safety of playing a character, so there is less social risk. There is a ton here that feels like a real poetry slam. It familiarizes them with the idea of competition and the notion that their art will be scored (even though art and storytelling are really tough to assign points to), while giving them the safety of taking on someone else's story. This is also a great way to figure out the needs of the new slam poets in your community as you work toward the possibility of them participating in a legitimate poetry slam as a culminating activity (if that fits for your community). It is preparation for pollination, and it allows you to see how comfortable your new slam poets are.

The following is a really solid example by Nathaniel, who chose to write a slam poem from the perspective of a Canadian cartoon character, Johnny Test. It's important to note here that the characters should have meaning and connection to those writing about them. I, personally, didn't know much about Johnny Test, but this student helped me learn about the character through his own understanding. Don't limit your new poets with your list of fictional characters; let them teach you a little something!

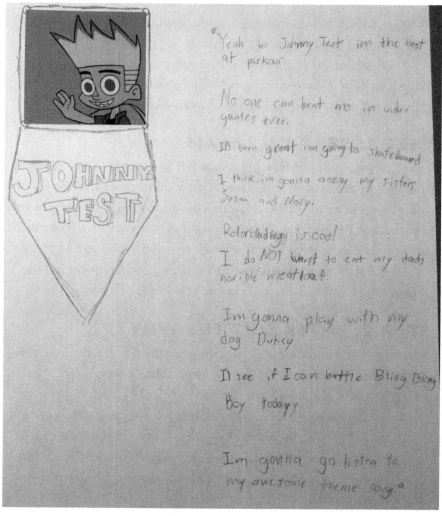

Nathaniel (Grade 4)

THIS IS SLAM POETRY

Slam poetry is a unique art form that mixes elements of storytelling, writing techniques, drama, rap battles, and so much more. Slam poetry is different from other forms of poetry because you are meant to see, hear, and feel the words of the poet as they speak them. You are meant to see their expression and hear their tone. That's why slam poetry ends up being something that is so individual in terms of experience: you are a unique human person experiencing the slam poetry work of another unique human person.

This assignment is about you. It is about what you like and why. Having an opinion is important, but being able to explain *why* you feel the way you do gives power and meaning to your opinions.

STEP 1: SEEK OUT SLAM

Your first job is to find some great slam poetry. Take the time to watch epic slam poets do their thing. You might want to go back to the list of poets I suggested in the first chapter or wait for more suggestions to come! Watch the pieces as they were meant to be seen, with all the small performance choices the slam poet made to make their poem what it is.

Watch slam poetry until you find a piece that makes you feel like, "Whoa, *that* is an awesome slam poem!"

STEP 2: WORK OUT THE WHY

It is essential to be able to explain why you feel the way you do about this slam poetry. This is intended to be a formal slam poetry study. Please answer the following questions:

1. What is the title of this slam poetry piece, and who is the author?
2. What do you think this slam poem is about? What message is the slam poet trying to get across? Please include at least *three* specific references from the slam poem itself that show why you feel this way.

3. Why do you like this slam poem? Again, please include at least *three* specific reasons why. Avoid things like "It's good," because that is too general. Were there specific lines that connected to you? Was there something about the way the poet performed their work? The more specific you are, the stronger your answers will be.

4. Slam poets are good at giving one another feedback that can help make their writing and performance stronger. Please use the strategy of "two stars and a wish," which means, if you could talk directly to the poet about this piece, what two specific things would you tell them they should keep, and what one specific thing would you tell them they could improve upon?

5. Who would you recommend this piece to and why? Who do you think needs to experience this piece, and what do you think they might take away or learn from it?

The way you have decided you want to plan for and build your new poet community plays a huge part in the ways you move toward the last chapter, in which I'll walk you through a variety of major community culminating activities. This is a great way to guide your poets toward creating their own culminating slam poetry piece.

Modifications: THIS Is Slam Poetry
Slam Activity—Pollination

Primary Challenge:

I tend to not use slam poetry in this activity modification. I have found that sometimes the content is a little too heavy. So what I like to do for little new poets is have them choose a book they love, either from the classroom or from home, then give it something I like to call a "high five plus one." With a high five plus one, I ask them to tell me why they like the story. They have to give me five specific reasons why they like the story, and they aren't allowed to use the word "good." If a poet slips up and uses that word, I help them out by asking what words could be better, different, or more specific. I ask things like, "What is it exactly that's good?" Next, I ask the little new poets what they think the book needs more of and what it could do better. I then do the same thing with a few poems the students can enjoy at their level, even taking the time to edit those poems into a new classroom version. This activity is all about creating opinions, thoughts, and feelings on poetry, so having both the language and the opportunity to do so is important.

Upping the Poetic Challenge:

First, I have students run the activity as it is built in the handout, but then I have them run the same activity together with the other slam poets in the room. As you're building toward these final big slam poetry moments, when pollination occurs and when things are blooming and growing, this is a good chance to take the pieces you're working on as culminating pieces and learn how to create positive feedback systems within the community.

Below is the bee badge that new slam poets can earn. I offer the bee badge to anyone who can prove they've contributed to the active inter-action and pollination of the poetry garden we've built together. Say, for example, they bring in a friend or show how they've used slam poetry to interact with someone outside of the immediate community; then they can ask for the pollinator badge (bee badge). Another great way to earn the pollinator (bee) badge is to go out and per-form outside of the community that you have built. Most of the time, this is for the new slam poets who are ready to take on the larger eco-system and let themselves grow into something strong and fruitful.

CHAPTER 5

BEARING FRUIT AND SEEDING THE WIND

"I DON'T THINK THEY'LL COME. IT'S NOT A BAS-KETBALL GAME."

I fell in love with slam poetry because when I was up there with those lights in my face the room so quiet I could hear every finger snap and every sound of agreement. I knew exactly when, where, and how to take my heart and tether it, for even a moment, to every other heart in the room. Admittedly, I am a very competitive person, so scoring well and winning mattered too. I trained hard. I spit poems in the car everywhere I went. It became a lullaby for my little ones in the back seat. I mumbled to myself at the gym. But I won. I won often. I became a name in my city and in my country. That felt great, and it allowed me to tour and work with so many poets of so many ages, and that's when my first love of being onstage evolved into the love of creating a stage under the feet of other poets.

To that end, I have spent countless hours building slams, poetry coffee houses, provincial and national festivals for both youth and youth-at-heart poets, video poetry projects that collaborated with film and music communities, visual poetry displays, ciphers, performances, gigs, and so much more. I joined local and national arts councils, and I was elected by my peers into all kinds of positions where I could develop and give more than I took. This is where I want to give you the tools to do the same, so you can fill your own poem with stories like these.

One of the times I was lucky enough to spend several days with a group of students, we decided together that our culminating event would be an evening poetry slam, so they could invite family and friends. The new slam poets were buzzing for days. They spent as much time writing, preparing, practicing, and editing their poetry as they did debating what kinds of snacks were the most poetic to serve and how they wanted to set up the audience's chairs. In all of that beautiful chaos, one young girl, a grade eight student, started to emerge as a leader. She was at every meeting. She was a champion of providing and receiving feedback on the poems that were growing. She prebaked cookies earlier on in the week to make sure the recipe was good enough for our poetry slam night. They were perfect, but I had to sample several anyway . . . for the sake of poetry. I'm an altruist like that.

On the night of our poetry slam, it wasn't a surprise that she was setting up and mumbling her poems to herself as she buzzed along in the work. We had collectively decided to make it a competitive slam, and she, as the leader she was becoming, was readying herself to be the queen bee of the night. As she and I were working, a few of her friends and fellow slam poets swung by to offer their assistance with sound equipment and general grunt work. One of them asked, "Can I save these seats for my parents? Or are you saving them for yours?"

The question visibly deflated her. She stopped working and rehearsing. She stopped seeming strong and ready. Her friends stared at her awkwardly until the word "no" pushed itself out like candle smoke. Her friends felt like they had done something wrong. The girl who asked about the chairs backpedaled, saying, "Listen, it's OK. You can have the chairs for your family; it's really not a big deal. I'm sorry." Queen Bee looked up, misty-eyed but holding strong, and said, "No, I'm sorry. You didn't do anything wrong. Just do what you want. I don't need to save any chairs for my family. I don't think they'll come. It's not a basketball game." And she walked out of the room with sunken shoulders. Her friends stayed behind to pick up the slack.

While we worked to set up, they explained to me that our queen bee had a family full of sports people. She had brothers who played basketball at a high level, and the family spent all of its time watching them play, going to local games, or watching together on TV. Basketball was their everything. She was the only person in the family without a sporty bone in her body, and it turned out that she'd been let down by her family before. They skipped drama performances in favor of playoffs. They missed concerts for practice. She felt like she didn't have any fans because she never got to wear a number on her back. Queen Bee knew this time would be no different. This slam poetry community would have to be her family tonight.

As we closed in on the start of our slam, Queen Bee came buzzing back, asking me for last-minute feedback and tips. I gladly agreed but used it as an opportunity to ask about the people she knew wouldn't come. She explained to me that they had been invited, that she'd given them a copy of the flyer she made for the event, and explained to them that she would be competing and intended to win. She told me that the response she got was, "What is that, a Thursday? I think the boys have a game." And that was it. She resigned herself to the fact that they wouldn't be coming.

People filed in, taking pictures with their slam poets and chatting, eating poetry slam snacks (like slam-wiches, which we thought was clever). We were moments away from starting, and Queen Bee hadn't even glanced at the door. Not once. Until we all had to. Everyone twisted their necks toward the door as a loud plastic trumpet, an airhorn, and fanatical hooting and hollering exploded in the hallway. As Queen Bee and the rest of the room looked on, a crowd of half a dozen people stormed into the room. They were dressed like they got lost on their way to a big game. Full school colors. Streamers. Banners. Posters. Face paint (a poetry slam first for me, I admit). They came in with thunderous energy, chanting and cheering like this was a game seven finals and their home team was about to take the championship. Smiles tore across the room, many mildly confused. This wasn't really how a poetry event was expected to unfold. Nobody had much of an idea as to why these out-of-place face-painted superfans had taken this detour on the way to the stadium. Nobody understood but Queen Bee, who was tearing up as she smiled and said, just above a whisper, "Dad. You guys came."

It was her family. All of them. They had arrived just in time, after their second bus was running late. They were all there for her. They poured themselves around her, creating a huddle and amping up their favorite poet. They seemed like an army, her army. Once the poetry slam began, they were quiet and supportive and paid their full respect to every slam poet who took the stage. But when their Queen Bee took the stage, they erupted. As she was called and approached the mic, they yelled, honked instruments, and shook the posters they'd made to support her. As she drew in a breath to start, they hushed, and you could feel every fiber of who they were listening to her intently. They were transfixed. When she finished, her last line hung in the room. Powerful. Everyone was quiet until her proud father yelled out, "That's my kid, the slam poet!"

The noise in that room rivaled the sound in some of the concert venues I've performed at. Queen Bee got all of the accolades she deserved as a leader, a slam poet, and a human being. She went on to win the slam that night, but more importantly, she felt she had won the right to be seen differently by her family. Afterward, her family was one of the only ones to stay and help clean, tear-smeared face paint and all. Her father came and extended his big bear paw of a hand out to me. "You must be the slam poet guy."

"People call me that often, yes. Some people also call me Mike."

"Listen, slam poet guy, I'll be honest (he looked over to make sure Queen Bee couldn't hear him), between you and me, I didn't have a hot clue what a poetry slam was, but it's important to her, so thank you. I love that slam poet. I love that kid."

I shook his hand as I pointed over his shoulder to his little queen bee across the room. As he turned to look over at her, crowded by peers and new fans telling her how incredible she was, she was only really looking at him, completely unaware of what he was saying to me, just beaming directly at her dad through it all.

"That," I said to him, "is a slam poet who absolutely knows how you love her."

Queen Bee also taught me a little something about developing community support on an individual level. Before this amazing moment, I created the opportunities I could for families, friends, and community members to be aware of and attend these events. Though this anecdote has a happy ending, it made me reflect on the potential anxiety new poets face when they're wondering who will come to support them. In following events, I sat with poets individually and asked them to make a "dream team" of support, as in, who would they want to have support them in an ideal situation. I then made efforts to call and email those names directly, where possible, and either invite them or, if they could not attend, make arrangements to record and share both the poet's performance and messages of support. Additionally, this allowed me to take stock of the family support that may or may not be available to those poets. Some would offer the names of friends or other trusted educators in the building. Letting those friends and teachers know how much they matter to those poets not only encouraged them to attend, but it created a sense of family support for new poets who may not have that at home, and it allowed me to teach them that family can take on all kinds of definitions. Part of the reason I love poetry so much is because it has the power to create a sense of connection and family for those who might not have it elsewhere. I have had many poets call their poetry slam team at school their family. It's one that is built around the value of their voices, around making the idea of family a conscious choice. Is there anything more meaningful than that?

This quilts together so much of what makes slam poetry a powerful experience. I love that the beauty and value of an individual voice is not lost but strengthened when mingled within a true community and the larger ecosystem. It creates a sense of belonging. Therein lies the intention of this chapter.

With bearing fruit and seeding the wind, I want this chapter to help you focus both on culminating events and creating a community of slam poets that could very well grow beyond whatever you had planned for your own experience. I've been lucky enough to work with kids in schools and later hear that they've got a thriving slam poetry team that sprang up through my work in their community. A culminating event or activity not only sets up motivation for those participating; it allows for a variety of opportunities for new slam poets to either finish their experience with closure or step into new leadership roles or personal identities. Some new slam poets will feel success and celebration within that finality; others will discover a sense of belonging in a new space that they had a hand in creating with their own voice. *That* is empowerment.

Community is something that wants to happen. We are, by nature, social animals. People want to feel like they belong to something, like they fit in and are wanted in that particular thing. These activities strengthen the bonds and shared experiences of your community. There will also be some learners who fall in love with slam poetry and want to make that into a community relationship of its own. There is a great book by Charles Vogl called *The Art of Community: Seven Principles of Belonging.* In it, Vogl talks about how there are four tentpoles to a healthy community. I believe when there is a culminating event or activity to work toward in poetry, there is also an inherent community that builds itself. The four principles of a healthy community are:

1. **Shared values:** As you're building a culminating event or activity that is made of real human people sharing their real human experiences, a value system is part of that process. What do we do as people to listen and support? What do safety and honesty look like for us as a collective? What is the identity of our slam poetry work within this group of valuable and unique voices? With a culminating event or activity, you'll be able to see which of your new slam poets are comfortable with this being their end point, as their bearing fruit, and which ones will see this as just a taste of a community they need more of.

2. **Membership identity:** Because of the nature of a culminating event or activity that values their individual voices and truth within that community standard, those who participate in a culminating event or activity build on their membership identity. The more moments and memories that are shared, the more a learner connects to their identity of the collective. Those who move forward as slam poets into performance and competition then become not only members but agents of that community.

3. **Moral prescriptions:** When you talk about what this community draws a hard line for (content, community action, etc.), it builds safety and connection and also strengthens the shared values discussed above. This works the same way those values do in developing and possibly evolving community through this slam poetry work.

4. **Insider understanding:** Finally, when you have a group of new slam poets who are developing, building, and presenting a meaningful culminating activity or event together, it makes your whole class feel like they're a part of something exclusive. They feel like they know about slam poetry and have a voice in ways others might not. The exact same thing can be said of any developing groups, only here with a deeper personal connection.

The intention of this chapter and this step in the journey is to celebrate one another through culminating experiences and acknowledge the ways in which the poetry work you've done has created community (bearing fruit), where you can look to what comes next (seeding the wind). Here, the end is the beginning and the end. Now, more than ever, you have the best idea of what celebration looks like for what you've built. You know now that the simplest way to value a whole person is to value their whole story. The intention of this chapter is to figure out what role poetry plays in that story and how to take the next steps for yourself and your new poets.

POET ACTIVITY: BEARING FRUIT AND SEEDING THE WIND (EDUCATOR SUPPORT)

STEP 1

Reflect. Giving themselves the chance to think about, celebrate, and build on all the good they've done is the reason writers were able to create the awesomeness of the *Teenage Mutant Ninja Turtles* movie and the uniquely different but wonderful *Teenage Mutant Ninja Turtles 2: The Secret of the Ooze*. Not taking the time to really think about the best next steps as a reaction to what had been most meaningful and valuable in earlier steps is the reason we have *Teenage Mutant Ninja Turtles 3*, which felt disconnected and didn't respect what came before it. It also included time travel for some reason. Reflecting on past events and planning the next steps are essential. It was the great poet and rapper Ice-T who put it best: "You better check yourself before you wreck yourself."

Remember, nobody is ever going to read this unless you show them. There is no better learning than making mistakes and evolving through them. What didn't work? What would you have done differently? What are you going to fail forward from?

_____

_____

_____

Now, flip that coin. (And don't worry about humility; remember, nobody is going to see this.) What did you do right? How did you absolutely rock the last chapter? Why are you an awesome new poet, and how did you help new poets germinate?

_____

_____

_____

STEP 2

Make a plan for your culminating event or activity!

Planning time is the right time to ask if what you're doing is P.O.E.Tree. In the last chapter, the intention was to think about ways to blur the lines and pollinate between the community you've built and the larger social ecosystem. This chapter puts you and your new poets at a crossroads in all of the most exciting and positive ways. Here at the culmination, you'll have a bunch of new poets who will feel satisfied with this being a fruit-bearing natural end point, and that's great. You'll have others who want this to be a step toward the life of taking on "slam poet" as part of their identity.

As an educator, you will be at a crossroads too. Do you want to finish this unit, then reflect and prep for something similar next year? Do you want to actively pursue a slam club or team in your school for the kids who really identify as slam poets? Do you want to seek out your local competitions and actively build those new poets into slam poets who compete and win and make you proud while you smile at the back of the room? There are no wrong answers, only big questions. The first of which is: How do we make sure we finish with the all-important echo of P.O.E.Tree?

P—**Pericardial:** As I mentioned, there are so many roads to consider for you and every new slam poet on their journey. The last chapter challenged you to show how close to the heart you keep the voices of your slam poets by finding ways to help others see their value and validate their voices as well. This chapter asks you to show how much you care, how close all of this (including your own truth) is to the heart of you, so you can support each new slam poet passionately, no matter what road they decide to take on their own poetic journey. Your pericardial self will ultimately empower them to speak their truth, both as poets and as people, because they know you hold their truth and journey close to your heart.

How are you going to make sure you show them you love and value their truth (and your own) enough to unconditionally support the journey they want for themselves? How are you going to make their choices clear and give them opportunities and options to bear their poetic fruit or become seeds in the wind? How will you balance the needs of those coming to the culmination of their slam poetry journeys with the needs of those who are not only finishing this chapter but already becoming leaders of the next?

I will. . .

○ —Open: One of my absolute all-time favorite words is "yet." It turns a negation into a commitment. For example: "I'm not good at cooking" establishes a defeatist attitude about cooking. "I'm not good at cooking *yet*" is a commitment to learning and getting better, perhaps breaking a few eggs until you stumble your way into being able to make a great omelet. In this chapter, I am asking you to be open to students' "yet." Believe that they have the power to become that incredible slam poet. Honestly, if you open yourself up to the "yet" of all the kids you teach, you give them limitless possibilities of what they can commit to being because they know you are open to seeing them as what they can be.

How will you make sure you are open to every new slam poet's vision for themselves as this adventure both culminates for some and evolves for others? How will you open yourself up to each individual new poet yet try to see them in the ways they envision themselves? How will you make sure you are open to every path, finale, and next possible verse?

I will. . .

E—**Electrifying:** This is the time to get electric. This will be the moment in building culminating activities and events when the student leaders will need your guidance and when your new slam poets will be preparing what they might see as their final piece. Others will really need your energy to get them to the finish line. But wait, there's more! Here's where your electricity is going to matter beyond your new slam poets. You're going to need to open up that mighty heart of yours and get others electrified about what these incredible kids and their voices are about to produce. If you've collectively decided to have a poetry slam, you need to find ways to get people excited about supporting and attending. If you've decided to do visual poetry, you might want to get people excited by putting together a film fest.

How are you going to make sure your new slam poets are electrified about the experience, no matter what it is and what their roles in it might be? How are you going to make sure the larger community, the larger ecosystem, is as excited about these kids and their slam poetry as you are?

I will . . .

T—**Tree:** I was lucky enough to do a TEDx talk on how science and poetry do the same job: they both try to figure out where we fit in the world and how we can actively and beautifully interact with it, contribute to it, and mean something within it. In that talk, I did a slam poem called "Butterfly Strong" about how community is something that feeds on, grows, and evolves through itself. Butterflies' wings seem fragile, but they are a complex overlap of scales that work together to create strength. We are lucky as educators to be living in this cyclical system that has new potential slam poets, new voices, and new stories arrive in our schools every year. Each student and story becomes a part of making the whole of what we practice stronger.

Will this be something you do again next year? Will you try to build a team or club with the leaders who have emerged? How will you make sure this is something that keeps growing and evolving beyond the culminating activity? How will you include students' voices in the decisions about how your community grows? How will you bring it to colleagues and welcome in new voices and perspectives?

I will. . .

_____

_____

_____

Things I want to remember when mapping this out (Notes to Self):

_____

_____

_____

STEP 3

So you've decided to throw a culminating event or activity into the mix. Ambitious! Fantastic! I believe wholeheartedly in the importance of a culminating event or activity. It allows those who need a finale to have one. It allows those who need confirmation and a stepping stone to the next level to have that. It allows you to finalize, breathe, celebrate your wins, and take a look at what the next round looks like in the ever-beautiful cyclical world of education we exist in.

Collaborative Storytelling

"I want to do a competitive poetry slam as my culminating event, but does making it competitive take away from the community aspect? Does it affect our ability to be collaborative storytellers?"

Brilliant question. Competition by nature can be divisive. Wanting to be the best at something can wake up feelings inside of us that make us want to be better than our fellow human people. I met some of my closest friends while competing against them, and we share a deep connection and bond, even after I absolutely obliterated them (I lost my fair share too). I've seen people who are as competitive as I am focus on the wins in those moments, then immediately become allies and friends as soon as they get off the stage.

Is making this competitive in opposition to the idea of collaborative storytelling? Heck no! Slam poetry is unique in its nature: it is literally presenting yourself to be judged numerically by peers and strangers. Those who go through it share a bond of understanding what that feeling is like. It is competition that breeds community and camaraderie through shared experience, respect, and intention. As is often yelled out at poetry slams, the point is not the points, the poetry is the point. I would add that the experience is too. I have participated in poetry slams from coast to coast, and I can't remember my numbers nearly as clearly as I do sitting around with other poets, talking about how we earned them.

There is also some responsibility in culmination to make sure you are collaboratively storytelling in terms of guiding students toward building something that is deeply personal yet has the quality to be presentable. Collaborative storytelling allows you to have the amazing role of collaborator and educator. How lucky are we to get to do what we do?

Emotional Mindfulness

"How do you make sure every person feels like a legitimate poet? How do you make sure this ends in positive and empowering ways for new slam poets who all have a variety of pathways and destinations?"

Again, great question. I like to think of Mister Rogers as one of the greatest slam poets of all time. Fred Rogers was all about giving people, mostly kids, a feeling that they were important and valued and that their feelings weren't something that needed to be buried but, rather, woven into their everyday human experience. To that end, he wrote little songs, had talks, and worded things in ways that simultaneously made the people around him feel connected to his story and valued in their own. That's slam poetry. Mister Rogers once said, "The world needs a sense of worth and will achieve it only by its people feeling that they are worthwhile." That is what I believe slam poetry gives to people: a forum and format to take their truth, engrave it into their voice, and feel their worth, knowing there is an audience that sees value in hearing it. Mister Rogers was right: the more each of us is worth, the more we are all worth together. That's the ticket of emotional mindfulness at this point. You need to know their hearts well enough to know what it would look like for each of them to see excellence and worth in themselves.

STEP 4

Buffet time!

If you're here from the first chapter wanting to begin your planning with the end in mind, some of this will be new and exciting, but trust me, it will all make sense when you travel from the beginning and work through the book with your new poets. This buffet has several choices for culminating events and activities. I would suggest focusing on one activity or event, because it will give you and your crew the chance to pour yourselves entirely into one great thing. Plus, you'll be asking for the support of the larger ecosystem, the outside community, and if you focus on one amazing event, you will get more support. It can be an evaluative piece or something you let your new poet leaders run, or a combination of both—whatever fits you and your team!

First, plan. These culminating activities and events won't just happen. Each requires details down to where and when, seating arrangements, microphones and technology, and who does what. Once you've planned, built, and hustled, all that's left is to host the event or implement the activity and watch as your new poets bloom. In that bloom, though, don't forget that it was the seeds you planted that made this possible. Allow yourself a moment to breathe this in.

But wait! There are a few additional things to consider in your development, which means there are a few additional things I'm happy to support you with.

1. How do you make your community universally accessible? It is important when you're building something that revolves around participation and active community engagement and involvement that you make sure it is accessible. Your new poets can (and should) come from all kinds of places and situations. Building with their diversity of need in mind is a huge step toward creating community success. Here are some simple ideas:

    - Have a variety of access points, both physical and in terms of participation levels. Get creative and thoughtful here. For example, there are two phenomenal Canadian poets, Saleem Hussain Ansari and John Hedderwick, who hosted a series of campfire poetry events where they livestreamed their poetry from campfires in national parks across the country. We live in a very technologically accessible time, in which they were able to use simple technologies to not only perform their poetry for people around the world from deep-woods campfires, but also invite others to participate open-mic style, without scoring or judgment, just support. Physically, your poetry community might have in-person meetings with online options through whatever streaming or meeting programs you are familiar and comfortable with. It might take the form of prerecorded and uploaded videos that other poets can access and comment on. Ask your new poets which programs they feel comfortable using to connect with one another. Leverage this information to create meaningful access points for everyone.
    - Check in often with new poets at all levels of involvement in your poetry community. Ask your leaders what their thoughts and feelings are on how new poets are engaging. Ask people who are newly involved how they're feeling about that involvement. Ask people who are coming as listeners if they'd like to be more active and how you

can make that possible. Yes, it is work to assure that there are many access points, both physical and virtual, but the more you work to hear people's needs and provide organic access points, the more your community will grow actively and exponentially.

- Make yourself a bloodhound for barriers. See if new poets are hindered by the physical time, space, or technology needed to participate. See if there are issues of language. It is fairly easy to find people who would be happy to "work" as translators or interpreters. They make great community members. There are also translation apps that have helped me build community with new poets I didn't share a language with. Time, anxiety, and social and personal situations can become barriers to new poets participating actively in something they might really need. Looking out for potential barriers allows you to build trust with the new poets as they become engaged community members.

2. How do you prioritize and support the performance aspects of slam-style poetry? Some of these aspects require you to focus on preparing your poets for both confidence and competence in front of a crowd. A few of the activities in this book will help with that, and below are some tips on how to help them put their best performance forward and engage with an audience. There should be a focus on the performing poet mindfully connecting with the audience, which looks like little things, such as looking up from their paper and knowing how to read the reactions of the room.

- Stress the importance of eye contact. Work on knowing where to look when the room is full or when you can't see anyone because of the lights. Little things like this matter in making an audience feel like you are there with them.
- Provide some tips and tricks on how they can project their voice and speak to the back of the room. Work with your

poets on how they can use body language to add to the story and the vibe of the performance. This is actually a phenomenal opportunity for pollination. Ask the drama and/or dance department in your school to bring their expertise to your new poets who are looking to enhance their performance skills. This also creates a bridge to other communities of performers, and that often leads to new members or supporters.

- Develop some tips and tricks for helping new poets deal with anxiety and nerves. Aside from providing them options that are not stage-based (like prerecording their work to be played at the event or creating a video poem), this is the best way you can help them grow in confidence and comfort though the performance aspects of poetry. There is so much opportunity here to create connection, trust, strategies, and confidence.

BUFFET

Welcome to the final helping! If you're joining us from earlier chapters to plan with the end in mind, kudos on your forethought, and welcome. These suggestions are meant to be larger-scale culminating activities or events. I would advise taking on just one and making it incredible. Go ahead and Frankenstein this smorgasbord. Make the most meaningful and authentic culminating activity or event you can for your slam poets based on whatever pieces fit best!

BUFFET BREAKDOWN
(ANOTHER OFFERING OF DELICIOUS ACTIVITIES)

1. **Visual/Video Slam Poem**—This is the culminating activity that doesn't necessarily require a set time and place. It will involve turning slam poetry into video poems, so working knowledge of and access to technology for filming and editing are important. Look for student leaders in this one!

2. **Slam Poetry Coffee House**—This is an event that will need a time and place, an audience, and a variety of little pieces to make it work. It is a chance for new slam poets to show off their work in an arena free of competition and formal numerical judgment. Also, there are typically snacks.

3. **Your Own Legit Competitive Poetry Slam**—This is an event akin to the one above. You'll need a time, a place, and an audience, but I'll also run through each step of running a legitimate competitive poetry slam with your new poet community! Snacks are optional here but fully supported by me.

4. **Hybrids**—I have also found success doing poetry coffee house nights that featured intermittent video poetry, so make sure you choose the options that fit your community best!

5. **Slam Poetry Teams/Clubs**—I will explain how to evolve this into a potential next step for slam poets.

These activities will include checklists that will provide planning steps for a presentation forum. This is the wrap party at the end! I'll also provide some tips on how to make this both the end and the beginning. With every poet and plant, once they mature, there is a point where they go forth and start seeding the next generation. This is a good opportunity for you to figure out how to grow this for the next school cycle. Are you going to include other educator colleagues and make your initial new poet community more extensive? Are you going to change some things for this new cycle to seed? Keep in mind that you won't be the only one seeding at the end of this. New slam poets will become accomplished in their own right and may become the leaders of the next wave, seeding and germinating the slam poetry in others.

One of my favorite ideas about poetry is that the best poetry is never actually finished, only abandoned for the sake of the next poem. Poetry can be infinitely edited, evolved, and grown. What if the growth of you and everyone around you wasn't abandoned? What if you were always looking to provide more chances to grow?

HOW TO CREATE VISUAL/VIDEO SLAM POETRY AS YOUR CULMINATING EVENT

STEP 1

Step one is to make sure this is the best fit for your new slam poets. Ask yourself if this feels right. Do you feel electrified about how this will look and feel for your community and the poets in it?

STEP 2

Now that you've determined which option is right for you, the next thing you'll need to decide is if you would like this to be something the new slam poets will upload and show to your local community or if you'll be having some kind of video slam poetry film fest night.

STEP 3

Spend time showing your new slam poets some amazing video poetry for inspiration. I typically have them jot down a few notes about what they liked about each piece and lead a classroom discussion about what makes a truly epic video poem (talk about visuals, music choices, inclusion of the poet and others, and much more!).

Here are some suggestions:

- "Jollof Rice" or "Right Side Up" by Ian Keteku
- "Look Up" by Gary Turk
- "Dear Future Generations: Sorry" by Prince Ea
- "Troll" or "To This Day Project" by Shane Koyczan
- "Ten Thousand Keys" by Mike Johnston (I made this one with some of my awesome new slam poets, and it stars my daughter when she was little!)
- "Become a Slam Poet in Five Steps" by Gayle Danley
- "A Poem That Will Change Your Perspective on Life" by Jon Jorgenson
- "Butterfly Boy" by Holly Painter

- "What Are We Fighting For?" by Andre Prefontaine
- "To Where the Trees Grow Tall" by Anis Mojgani

Challenge your new slam poets to find poems they like and are inspired by. It is important to take a moment to break down the why. Why are these great? How do these poets get their messages across visually? What aspects make it work?

This is also a great place to integrate classic pieces of poetry that have been made into visuals. I typically use something like Maya Angelou's "Still I Rise." That poem reminds them that they'll rise above what hiccups they're about to go through in the creation process.

STEP 4

Create. Now is the time to let your new slam poets get their writing in for their final pieces. Help them create with the end in mind. In this case, that looks like video poetry, so they'll have to think about how to make a great visual impact at the same time. Create a video poem of your own alongside them, as my own poets challenged me to do with "Ten Thousand Keys." It's also important that you give all of your new slam poets the same submission criteria. Make them aware that they all get the same three-minute time frame. That's it!

STEP 5

This next step can go in several directions, depending on what you and your new slam poets have decided is your endpoint.

- Set a date for each step that is appropriate for your new slam poet community (writing, editing, storyboarding, filming and editing, uploading, and presenting).
- If you're going to present your videos in a community, you'll have to decide how that will look. I suggest choosing a space that is atypical to their daily routine (like a library) and creating a special moment for your slam poetry film festival.
- Outside of that, you'll need to figure out exactly the time, place, cost (rental/entry; I often "charge" a donation of canned goods

for those able to make one). You'll have to talk with the leaders in your community about advertising, special invites (to your administration and fellow educators), and—this is paramount—you'll need to choose and train a fantastic host for the event and let them lead guests through this experience. Each piece will feel very different, so the host is important in resetting the energy of the room and getting people ready for the next piece.

STEP 6

Enjoy the night. Embrace it. I have run countless events like this; some with a handful of new slam poets sharing their video work for one another over cookies, and others where hundreds showed up to support and watch. Not one time have I ever had an event go as planned. Remember when we talked about the beautiful concept of wabi-sabi? Some of my favorite slam poetry film fest events include "the one where the sound system shut down, so one of the parents who was a part-time DJ brought his equipment from home and we ended the night with an impromptu dance party" and "the one where the school had a power failure, so we used a multitude of long power cords from a house a half block away to project the videos onto the side of the building." That's part of the magic.

STEP 7

It is always important to take the time for feedback and reflection. After the event or activity is over, take the time not just to celebrate but have an honest chat with your new slam poets about the entire experience. Look for leaders here. In my experience, they tend to appear through these events and are more than ready to spread the seeds of the poetry community.

HOW TO CREATE A SLAM POETRY COFFEE HOUSE AS YOUR CULMINATING EVENT

STEP 1

Step one is making sure this is the best fit for your new slam poets. Ask yourself if it feels right. Do I feel electrified about how this will look and feel for our community? This is a noncompetitive option; it will have more of a structured open-mic feel. A smaller open-mic scenario allows you to create a small-scale ambiance. For example, a smaller venue allows for physical closeness and enhanced intimacy with the audience.

STEP 2

If you've determined that a slam poetry coffee house is the right option, you'll have to decide on the who, what, where, when, and how (we already know celebrating amazing new slam poets and their work is the why). Choose a location and time, ask your leaders and those who are helping you what you will physically need (snacks and audio equipment, for example), and decide who you want to invite. Problem-solve. Ask important questions, like who is bringing the coffee to the coffee house, should hot chocolate be an option, have you booked a venue that will provide things like this, or are you building your own coffee house in a venue like your school library? In short, make a solid game plan.

STEP 3

This is the moment to show your poets other artists to inspire them. Show them Buddy Wakefield and Andre Prefontaine. Show them Andrea Gibson and Beau Sia. Show them Saul Williams and Sarah Kay, George Watsky and Patrick Roche. Take time to expose them to great work because great work is both inspiring and shows what they can evolve into.

STEP 4

Create. Now is the time to let your new slam poets build their most exceptional work, as they know they're headed to the culmination. There is a slam poetry rule that poets have to live by three-minute time limits. That's a pretty solid span of time to give them. I also think it's important for you to create at the same time. Challenge yourself to develop and present work alongside your poets! I have seen educators put this into practice, and it is absolute magic.

STEP 5

Now you will be working with your new slam poets to edit their work, workshop, rehearse, and think about presenting. Some may even want to memorize, which is a high-level slam poetry skill but not mandatory. They should be focusing on their presentation and their process. Slam poetry is meant to be presented and experienced like live theatre. Help them dive in!

You and your team will be working on the details of the actual physical event, deciding on things like time, place, and cost. Again, I sometimes "charge" canned food entry, if it's appropriate. You'll have to talk with the new slam poets on your planning team about things like how to advertise, special invites (administrators and your fellow educators!), and selecting and training an awesome host(s) for your event. Each piece will feel different, so a host is very important for resetting the energy of the room.

STEP 6

Enjoy it. You deserve it, and so do all the new slam poets who are going to be brave enough to put themselves out there. Read step six of the previous activity (Visual/Video Slam Poetry) for a little more insight about and appreciation for wabi-sabi. This is a chance to show excitement in your greater ecosystem, an opportunity to seed the wind and see where those seeds germinate. Let these seeds become planted in as many other classrooms and hearts as possible. Make your entire school P.O.E.Tree.

STEP 7

Take the time for feedback and reflection, as always.

HOW TO CREATE YOUR OWN LEGITIMATE COMPETITIVE POETRY SLAM AS YOUR CULMINATING EVENT

STEP 1

I'm really proud of you for going all-in on a competitive poetry slam. Step one is to look over the previous activity of creating your own slam poetry coffee house. At its core, a poetry slam is a coffee house with the added fun of competition! Your job will be to look through the planning of the coffee house format and prepare to use that as your principal guide.

STEP 2

Build the structure of your slam. I will be using the National Poetry Slam rules and regulations as they have been adopted by SpeakNORTH, the official governing body of all poetry slams in Canada. They are responsible for the development and structure of national-level competitions that start in local cities and work toward a variety of formal poetry slams for individual and team slam poets every year. I will be taking excerpts from their documents (with permission, I promise!) to help you. The following instructions are for running the actual slam within the coffee house activity format.

Choosing the right host(s) for the night is important. That host will have to stay unbiased as the others compete; they are not going to compete themselves, but they'll have the responsibility of resetting and keeping up the energy of the crowd in between competing slam poets. There isn't any kind of special magic to this. A host capable of conversing with the audience will naturally become a palate cleanser between poets. You will need to select someone who is OK with not competing. Explain the position and look for volunteers or ask someone outside of the slam poet community to host so everyone who wants to can still compete.

- Choose a sacrificial or calibration poet ahead of time. They will get scores, but those scores will only be a way for judges to figure out how to score and for the host(s) to practice resetting them in between. This is perfect for a new slam poet who wants to see what their scores might be but doesn't want the pressure of formally competing.

Each bout will have a sacrificial poet (also known as a calibration poet), selected by the Slam Master or their delegate, to calibrate the judges. The sacrificial poet will perform before the official competition begins and will receive scores from the judges as if they are a part of the competition.

You will also need to choose both a scorekeeper and a timekeeper. These can be absolutely anyone who can write down numbers and use a stopwatch. They also cannot be competitive poets for obvious reasons. These volunteers have a very important role, as they will be the keepers of the means of winning. Both the score and the calculation of time penalties are important. You will take on the role of Slam Master for the evening. This means you are the keeper of the rules and the scores. It is your job to make sure the poets follow the rules, and that scores and penalties are accurate. Any arguments, challenges, and discrepancies will also have to come through you. You also get to call yourself Slam Master for a night, so that's awesome.

1. First, you will have to choose five judges. Those judges must be as impartial as possible. That means you should avoid judges who have connections and biases toward any of the slam poets. One way I avoid searching for judges the night of and worrying about bias is by specifically inviting "celebrity" poetry slam judges. These can be administrators, superintendents, local radio personalities, local slam poets, librarians, or whoever you'd like! I find that advertising "celebrity" guest judges gets everyone a little more excited as well. I've had politicians, relatively famous actors, weather people, and professional sports folks show up to be judges.

2. Before the event begins, write the names of the competing poets on slips of paper and place them in a container. During the competition, the host(s) will draw a new name from the container as each competitor is called up. Participation must be random.

3. Once everyone is ready and your five judges are present with a means of writing down their scores (I suggest a handheld dry erase board for each), have the host(s) start the night! Here is a brief outline of what they should say (it's a loose list, so make it specific to your event!)

    a. <u>Intro:</u> Host(s) introduce themselves, briefly explain the concept, and introduce the judges and any special guests.

    b. <u>Rules:</u> Host(s) go over the formal rules of the poetry slam as a reminder to both the slam poets and the audience. Here are the scripted rules for SpeakNORTH hosts at formal events:

        "Scores for each performance will be given by five judges selected before the bout begins (point out judges). All scores are on a scale from 0.0 to 10.0, in increments of tenths. The poet's highest and lowest scores are dropped and the three middle scores added together for a final score out of 30.0.

        "Poems must be no longer than three minutes in duration. Each performer receives a 10-second grace period beyond three minutes. Every 10 seconds thereafter (or portion of 10 seconds thereafter) will be penalized with a 0.5 point deduction. For example, at 3:10, there is a time penalty of 0.5 points. At 3:20, there is a time penalty of a full point. All time penalties will be announced immediately after scores are recorded.

        "The time starts when a poet engages the audience. The time stops when the performance clearly ends. This includes any speaking or physically interacting with the audience.

"No props, music, nudity, or costumes are allowed in the competition. There is a 2.0 point penalty for any prop, costume or music (not made by the slam poet using their own body) and immediate disqualification for any other infractions. Poets may read from paper or handheld digital devices (smartphones, etc.).

"Competitors may perform (in any way they see fit) a solo piece when called to the stage, or they may choose a team piece, which must either be primarily written by the artist in question, or must be cooperatively written by artists in the piece.

"Slam hosts will conduct themselves as neutrally as possible at all times during bouts.

"Any disagreements, complaints, or protests from a bout will be handled by the Slam Master."

c. Host(s) will tell the audience about the concept of "snaps."

d. Hosts will then explain what a sacrificial or calibration poet is and invite that poet to come up, perform, and be scored.

They'll read each score aloud, making sure the score-keeper has each score so they can calculate. The host(s) will then double-check with the timekeeper that there are no time penalties. Host(s) can encourage the audience to audibly agree or disagree with scores.

e. After the sacrificial poet has done their work, the host(s) will take the container with the names in it, talk the crowd through, and calm them down, then choose the first slam poet at random. This poet will immediately come up, and once they interact with the audience, their three-minute time begins.

f. After each slam poet performs, the host(s) will give the judges one minute to write their scores. They'll count down and have the judges show their scores simultaneously. They will then read the scores aloud for the scorekeeper to write them down. The host(s) will then check for time penalties.

g. Repeat until every participating slam poet has had the opportunity to slam.

h. Once all poets have slammed and been scored, the host(s) will speak to and thank the audience for the evening while the final scores are calculated. Once they are calculated, the host(s) will announce the top five poets, starting from five and going all the way to the slam champ! (It is your choice whether to have a prize or prizes.)

i. The host(s) will thank everyone for coming and invite them to help stay and clean up! You did it! You and your crew made it through your formal competitive poetry slam!

STEP 3

Step three is reflection and celebration. You've earned it! On the following pages, I've provided copyable pages for poet scoring, as well as for calculating time penalties.

Time	Penalty
3:10 and under	no penalty
3:10.01–3:20	-0.5
3:20.01–3:30	-1.0
3:30.01–3:40	-1.5
3:40.01–3:50	-2.0
and so on	[-0.5 for every 10 seconds over 3:10]

A chart explaining time penalties (based on a 10-second grace period)

Name of Poet	Score 1	Score 2	Score 3	Score 4	Score 5	Total Time	Time Penalty	Total Score (out of 30)

HOW TO CREATE YOUR OWN HYBRID POETRY SLAM CULMINATING EVENT

STEP 1

Read the previous options for culminating events and activities. Look for pieces you feel excited about.

STEP 2

Pick and develop whatever hybrid you feel fits your community best. Here are just a few variations I've done and had success with that you might want to consider!

- A competitive video poetry slam where slam poets present their video poems in different classes to get students' votes. This activity got the student body so excited that it prompted a video slam poetry club.
- A slam poetry coffee house that features video slam poetry projected in between slam poetry presentations. We held it in a library, and we switched between live slam performances and video poems. (I've also done the same for a competitive poetry slam with an amazing video poetry finale.)
- I once had a group where half wanted to compete and half wanted to just perform, so we had a competitive slam with "palate cleanser" slam poets in between.
- I did a "Poetry Slam on the Road" where we actually went to other schools to perform these slam poetry pieces. The poets felt like rock stars.

HOW TO CREATE A SLAM POETRY CLUB AFTER THE CULMINATING EVENT

STEP 1

The first step is to breathe, reflect, and figure out which of the new slam poets need more and which are ready to evolve into leaders.

STEP 2

To steal a quote like I'm stealing third base, "If you build it, they will come." You'll need to decide on a consistent time and place to meet. Once you've set up your first meeting, make sure you're making it P.O.E. Tree. Be waiting with open arms and an open heart for anyone who shows up, whatever their motivation. They're there because they need to be.

STEP 3

Now that you're meeting, you'll need to collectively figure out your why. Are you trying to find a way to be competitive? If so, what is locally available for you? Are you getting together to write, create, and share with one another? Will you be naming your team, making a logo, printing shirts, or presenting at school assemblies?

It also helps to have a process for each week. I suggest beginning with sharing and feedback, some kind of writing activity, then the homework of writing something to share for the next week's team meeting. The possibilities are endless.

Included is a badge that I often use. Decide if it fits your community's journey. It's a stylized seed that, when put up on the wall, looks like drifting seeds in the wind.

AFTERWORD:

SEEDLINGS IN THE SHADE OF THE TREES

I know I usually start with a quote and a charming anecdote. I won't do that here because, especially now, it's not about my story anymore. It's about yours. It's about the voice and the story of your new poets. It's about the stories and stanzas you've now shared together. That's one of the most incredible pieces in all of this. You'll have worked with these exceptional new poets as they found the power behind their story and learned how to speak their truth. You will be able to look them each in the eye and know them more deeply because you've valued and empowered their voices. Your stories, the poems that each and every one of you is writing, now have stanzas that feature one another.

That's one of the things I love the most about being an educator: we are in the business of people, and we become a part of their story as much as they become a part of ours. It is a privilege and a responsibility. You are poetry. You are a poet who has agency in your own story and how it is told. I hope you let yourself see just how valuable that makes you, how irreplaceable that makes your voice. Once you see that in yourself, I believe it makes it impossible not to see that worth in the people around you.

I'm so thankful to you for taking the time to show yourself and the people around you the importance of the poem you write just by being you every day. Whatever you have done with this book to make it your own, thank you. Thank you for caring enough to see yourself in a new light and shine that light on the people around you. I hope you see this end as a beginning and allow yourself to dream big about what you can do with new poets who might want to become the same seed for others that you were for them. I hope you feel like you understand the new poets and yourself a little better through all of this. But above all, I hope that from here on, whenever you see a student or a colleague or yourself in a reflective surface, there is a piece of you that can't help but hear the echo of the singular truth: you are poetry.

GLOSSARY OF DOPE SLAM POETRY TERMS TO UPGRADE YOUR COOL

Biting: Slang for the accusation that one poet has stolen material from another without giving due credit.

Curse you, linear time: Often delivered at high volumes by a collective or crowd, this indicates displeasure with time penalties. It shows support to a slam poet who has taken a time penalty.

Cipher: Formally meaning both a secret code and a zero, a cipher is when a group of slam poets meet together outside of official competition and perform slam poetry without a numerical score.

Go in, poet: Typically directed at a slam poet who is about to perform, it is a means to encourage them to dive completely into their performance.

Penultimate: Meaning second to last, often used by hosts of poetry events to indicate when things are the second to last in the most poetic way.

Piece: The common name for a slam poem.

Poemcee: An endearing term used to describe the host or emcee of a slam poetry event.

Score Creep: The phenomenon in which scores increase as a poetry slam event progresses and judges become more connected to and inspired by the atmosphere. It is to be avoided.

Show Love: This expression is a simple call to demonstrate appreciation for the work that the slam poet has produced.

Snaps: The act of snapping one's fingers, which replaces clapping, during a poet's performance as a means of showing support in specific moments. "Earning one's snaps" is the act of performing well.

Speak your truth: A reminder to the slam poet that this is their story and it is important for them to maintain their truth.

Spit fire: This term indicates that a slam poet is either about to or has previously delivered slam poetry work that is meaningful and/ or effective.

Streetlights are on: A term geared toward slam poets about to perform, reminding them that the lights are on them, which indicates that they have both the stage lights and the attention of those gathered.

Team piece: This is a slam poetry piece in which one slam poet is the primary writer, but they enlist the aid of others for the performance of the piece.

The point is not the points: A reminder that the scores are not the main motivation for creating and performing meaningful and worthwhile slam poetry pieces.

Video poem: This is a slam poem that has been made into a film with specific consideration for visual storytelling.

ABOUT THE AUTHOR

Like you, Mike Johnston is a poet.

He is an award-winning classroom teacher, spoken-word artist, and poetry advocate and educator. He has toured and performed internationally as a champion slam poet, having won myriad slam poetry titles at provincial and national levels. He has consistently used his travel for performance touring and poetry slam competition as a Trojan horse. At every destination he has workshopped, trained, and created opportunities for poetry education with innumerable students and educators around the world.

He is a poetry-community builder, having held and been elected to titles such as slam master, founder, and director at a variety of festivals and slam poetry organizations with a focus on new poets and youth poetry education. Helping others find and build their poetic voices has become the heartbeat of his motivation. He was named a National Geographic Grosvenor Teacher Fellow, which feeds his passion for living stories, seeking the stories and poetry of others as well as his inclination toward adventuring. He has written, taught, and workshopped poetry on beaches with sea lions and waist deep in water surrounded by sea turtles, and he cannot wait to keep traveling down every road less traveled that poetry brings his way.

MORE FROM
DAVE BURGESS
Consulting, inc.

Since 2012, DBCI has published books that inspire and equip educators to be their best. For more information on our titles or to purchase bulk orders for your school, district, or book study, visit DaveBurgessConsulting.com/DBCIbooks.

More from the *Like a PIRATE*™ Series

Teach Like a PIRATE by Dave Burgess
eXPlore Like a PIRATE by Michael Matera
Learn Like a PIRATE by Paul Solarz
Play Like a PIRATE by Quinn Rollins
Run Like a PIRATE by Adam Welcome
Tech Like a PIRATE by Matt Miller

Lead Like a PIRATE™ Series

Lead Like a PIRATE by Shelley Burgess and Beth Houf
Balance Like a PIRATE by Jessica Cabeen, Jessica Johnson, and Sarah Johnson
Lead beyond Your Title by Nili Bartley
Lead with Appreciation by Amber Teamann and Melinda Miller
Lead with Culture by Jay Billy
Lead with Instructional Rounds by Vicki Wilson
Lead with Literacy by Mandy Ellis

Leadership & School Culture

Culturize by Jimmy Casas
Escaping the School Leader's Dunk Tank by Rebecca Coda and Rick Jetter

Fight Song by Kim Bearden

From Teacher to Leader by Starr Sackstein

If the Dance Floor Is Empty, Change the Song by Joe Clark

The Innovator's Mindset by George Couros

It's OK to Say "They" by Christy Whittlesey

Kids Deserve It! by Todd Nesloney and Adam Welcome

Let Them Speak by Rebecca Coda and Rick Jetter

The Limitless School by Abe Hege and Adam Dovico

Live Your Excellence by Jimmy Casas

Next-Level Teaching by Jonathan Alsheimer

The Pepper Effect by Sean Gaillard

Principaled by Kate Barker, Kourtney Ferrua, and Rachael George

The Principled Principal by Jeffrey Zoul and Anthony McConnell

Relentless by Hamish Brewer

The Secret Solution by Todd Whitaker, Sam Miller, and
Ryan Donlan

Start. Right. Now. by Todd Whitaker, Jeffrey Zoul, and
Jimmy Casas

Stop. Right. Now. by Jimmy Casas and Jeffrey Zoul

Teachers Deserve It by Rae Hughart and Adam Welcome

Teach Your Class Off by CJ Reynolds

They Call Me "Mr. De" by Frank DeAngelis

Thrive through the Five by Jill M. Siler

Unmapped Potential by Julie Hasson and Missy Lennard

When Kids Lead by Todd Nesloney and Adam Dovico

Word Shift by Joy Kirr

Your School Rocks by Ryan McLane and Eric Lowe

Technology & Tools

50 Things You Can Do with Google Classroom by Alice Keeler and
Libbi Miller

50 Things to Go Further with Google Classroom by Alice Keeler and
Libbi Miller

140 Twitter Tips for Educators by Brad Currie, Billy Krakower, and Scott Rocco

Block Breaker by Brian Aspinall

Building Blocks for Tiny Techies by Jamila "Mia" Leonard

Code Breaker by Brian Aspinall

The Complete EdTech Coach by Katherine Goyette and Adam Juarez

Control Alt Achieve by Eric Curts

The Esports Education Playbook, by Chris Aviles, Steve Isaacs, Christine Lion-Bailey, and Jesse Lubinsky

Google Apps for Littles by Christine Pinto and Alice Keeler

Master the Media by Julie Smith

Reality Bytes by Christine Lion-Bailey, Jesse Lubinsky, and Micah Shippee, PhD

Sail the 7 Cs with Microsoft Education by Becky Keene and Kathi Kersznowski

Shake Up Learning by Kasey Bell

Social LEADia by Jennifer Casa-Todd

Stepping Up to Google Classroom by Alice Keeler and Kimberly Mattina

Teaching Math with Google Apps by Alice Keeler and Diana Herrington

Teachingland by Amanda Fox and Mary Ellen Weeks

Teaching Methods & Materials

All 4s and 5s by Andrew Sharos

Boredom Busters by Katie Powell

The Classroom Chef by John Stevens and Matt Vaudrey

The Collaborative Classroom by Trevor Muir

Copyrighteous by Diana Gill

CREATE by Bethany J. Petty

Ditch That Homework by Matt Miller and Alice Keeler

Ditch That Textbook by Matt Miller

Don't Ditch That Tech by Matt Miller, Nate Ridgway, and
  Angelia Ridgway
EDrenaline Rush by John Meehan
Educated by Design by Michael Cohen, The Tech Rabbi
The EduProtocol Field Guide by Marlena Hebern and Jon Corippo
The EduProtocol Field Guide: Book 2 by Marlena Hebern and
  Jon Corippo
Game On? Brain On! by Lindsay Portnoy, PhD
Innovating Play by Jessica LaBar-Twomy and Christine Pinto
Instant Relevance by Denis Sheeran
LAUNCH by John Spencer and A.J. Juliani
Make Learning MAGICAL by Tisha Richmond
Pass the Baton by Kathryn Finch and Theresa Hoover
Project-Based Learning Anywhere by Lori Elliott
Pure Genius by Don Wettrick
The Revolution by Darren Ellwein and Derek McCoy
Shift This! by Joy Kirr
Skyrocket Your Teacher Coaching by Michael Cary Sonbert
Spark Learning by Ramsey Musallam
Sparks in the Dark by Travis Crowder and Todd Nesloney
Table Talk Math by John Stevens
Unpack Your Impact by Naomi O'Brien and LaNesha Tabb
The Wild Card by Hope and Wade King
The Writing on the Classroom Wall by Steve Wyborney

Inspiration, Professional Growth & Personal Development

Be REAL by Tara Martin
Be the One for Kids by Ryan Sheehy
The Coach ADVenture by Amy Illingworth
Creatively Productive by Lisa Johnson
Educational Eye Exam by Alicia Ray
The EduNinja Mindset by Jennifer Burdis
Empower Our Girls by Lynmara Colón and Adam Welcome
Finding Lifelines by Andrew Grieve and Andrew Sharos

The Four O'Clock Faculty by Rich Czyz

How Much Water Do We Have? by Pete and Kris Nunweiler

P Is for Pirate by Dave and Shelley Burgess

A Passion for Kindness by Tamara Letter

The Path to Serendipity by Allyson Apsey

Sanctuaries by Dan Tricarico

Saving Sycamore by Molly B. Hudgens

The SECRET SAUCE by Rich Czyz

Shattering the Perfect Teacher Myth by Aaron Hogan

Stories from Webb by Todd Nesloney

Talk to Me by Kim Bearden

Teach Better by Chad Ostrowski, Tiffany Ott, Rae Hughart, and Jeff Gargas

Teach Me, Teacher by Jacob Chastain

Teach, Play, Learn! by Adam Peterson

The Teachers of Oz by Herbie Raad and Nathan Lang-Raad

TeamMakers by Laura Robb and Evan Robb

Through the Lens of Serendipity by Allyson Apsey

The Zen Teacher by Dan Tricarico

Children's Books

Beyond Us by Aaron Polansky

Cannonball In by Tara Martin

Dolphins in Trees by Aaron Polansky

I Want to Be a Lot by Ashley Savage

The Princes of Serendip by Allyson Apsey

Ride with Emilio by Richard Nares

The Wild Card Kids by Hope and Wade King

Zom-Be a Design Thinker by Amanda Fox

Made in the USA
Middletown, DE
21 April 2021

38157277R00126